Uphill All The Way

By James Sloter

D1316175

AUTHOR'S FAMILY, 1943
Father (32), Sandra (3 months), Mother (28)
James (8), Donald (5), Julian (7)

First printing—October 2003
Second printing—January 2004

ISBN: 0-9748333-0-4

Additional copies of this book are available by mail.
Send a check for $12.95 + $3.95 shipping and handling (Iowa Residents add 7% sales tax) to:

Goldenrod Press
PO Box 71
Algona, Iowa 50511.
515-295-7090

Printed in the United States by Morris Publishing
3212 East Highway 30
Kearney, NE 68847
1-800-650-7888

I dedicate this book to my parents, Bill and Lela Sloter. Both are now deceased, but they live on in our memory.

Lela, at age 17   Bill, at age 24

Acknowledgements

I would not have been able to write this book without the encouragement and help of my dear mother, Lela Sloter, now deceased. Many of the stories are hers. Her ability to clearly recall details of her life, and of our family life, amazed me. I also want to thank my loving wife, Marsha, for her patience and suggestions as she read and re-read each vignette; my brother, Julian, who helped clarify many details and did repeated editing for me; and Ella Zumach, a good friend and retired English teacher, who also gave freely of her time and talent to encourage me and to edit my work. Thank you also to Illena Sletten, and Oakley & Charlene Sloter who provided critical information about our ancestors, which made further research possible and to Mark Shoesmith for his help with Sloter family details.

INTRODUCTION

My name is James — James Sloter. They call me Jim. I am the oldest of five children born to Bill Sloter and Lela (Jackson) Sloter. I was born January 24, 1935, in a farmhouse on the "home place", located between the towns of Corwith and Kanawha, Iowa. I am now retired and live with my wife, Marsha, in the small Midwestern town of Algona, Iowa.

But this book, entitled **Uphill All the Way,** is not about me. It is about my Dad and Mom, two incredibly focused, determined, resourceful and hard-working people — one very tough, with keen survival instincts and a raucous sense of humor (my Dad), and the other always humble, caring and self-sacrificing (my Mom). For over fifty-eight years, they were a "team". Theirs is a remarkable story.

My father, one of fourteen children and a "survivor" in the truest sense of the word, suffered ill health the last twelve years of his life. Because he was essentially "shut in" during that time, I visited him whenever possible. As we talked, sometimes for hours, he told me stories about his life and related many of his life experiences. Through that time together, I learned a lot about Dad and the circumstances that helped to form his character. I believe he told me things that he had kept to himself for over sixty years. They are included in these writings.

My mother, a twin, lost her father when she was age eleven. Life immediately got very difficult. My grandfather was a farmer and was farming 160 acres near the small rural community of Kanawha when he died. At the time of his death, he was preparing to move to a larger farm (240 acres) between Kanawha and Corwith. My grandmother was suddenly left to raise seven children on her own – a son, James, the eldest, and six daughters – and to somehow find a way to run the farm. That experience, of growing up on the farm without a father, affected how my Mom thought about everything throughout her life, and also helped her to develop into the very special person that she became. She was hard-working, fiercely loyal and, although slight of stature, was extremely tenacious and long-suffering. She had a strong constitution – and certainly needed one to put up with my father's shenanigans and some of the circumstances he created!

Dad and Mom lived at a time in our history when everything was a struggle — getting an education, getting a job, raising a family, paying the bills — just getting by. Their whole life seemed to revolve around looking for work, scrounging to pay the bills and providing for their family.

I have chosen to tell this story through a series of vignettes, all true stories, some of which involve my siblings and me -- but most of which shed light on the lives of our parents, both individually and collectively, and on the life of our family.

This is a story of triumph. Dad passed away on February 22, 1993, leaving behind a rich legacy for his family to build upon. As noted, he was a survivor — and, in his own way, that is what he taught us — how to be personally resourceful and to take responsibility for ourselves and for our families.

Mom was still alive when this was written, but has since passed away. She was eighty-six when she died on September 25, 2001. She lived alone in her home in Corwith, Iowa, about twenty miles southeast of Algona. We cherish her memory and her positive influence on our lives. As you will see, she was the softer, gentler half of the partnership — but equally determined and committed to our family goals. Her children all share her values and never wanted to do anything that would "let her down". I thoroughly enjoyed the many hours that Mom and I spent together on these writings.

Mom and Dad both believed in us and expected a lot from us — that was always understood. And, as far as we were concerned, that was all that mattered. Their belief in us was very instrumental in our success, both while we were at home and when we became adults.

Writing this book has truly been a labor of love. As I recount some of our life experiences, it brings back memories that still touch me deeply. Indeed, if you enjoy reading this book even a small fraction as much as I have enjoyed writing it, I will consider it a big success. Thank you for joining my family and me on this trip back through the years.

PROLOGUE

Our Heritage

The land of our ancestors, Ostfriesland, Germany, is flat as far as the eye can see in all directions. Located in the northwest corner of Germany and bordered on three sides by the North Sea, it is low-lying "polder" land, reclaimed from the North Sea and protected by dikes. Barriers constructed to break up ocean waves prevent water erosion on the approximately twenty-foot high dikes. Water that manages to seep into the lowlands and excess rainwater are pumped out into the sea. That was done with rows of large "Dutch windmills" years ago, but is now done with huge diesel-powered auger pumps.

There are moors, or marshland, in the central part of Ostfriesland. Colonists began settling the poorly-drained land, containing peat bogs, in 1767. The new arrivals knew nothing of how to properly drain the moors and sank deep into the marshland. They lived in miserable conditions and did what they could to eek out a living. Using natural resources available to them, they built houses or huts from peat turf, or from sticks and straw mixed with mud. Their houses were very small, containing minimal room for the people and their animals. The walls separating the house from the barn were often left open at the top to allow warmth from the animals to enter the living area.

In addition to being used to construct houses and other buildings, the coarse grass found in the moors was harvested and used to weave doormats and to make brushes and pot cleaners, which they sold door to door throughout Ostfriesland. If sales didn't go well, they often resorted to begging.

Special footwear was needed to keep their feet warm and dry. Their choice was wooden shoes. If the marsh was very deep, they would fasten leather "uppers" to them, creating warm, watertight boots.

A village was eventually established in the moors and was named Moordorf. The large number of children born to the colonists made the poverty there even worse. At one time, it was said that Moordorf had more children than any other village in Germany.

The feelings resulting from the miserable living conditions these people endured, and the time required to learn what was needed to drain the moors, has been summarized this way by the people now living in the area: "The first generation living in the moors said it was their death, the second their need, and the third their bread."

My paternal great grandmother, Tatje Hinricks Wilts, was born into those conditions near Moordorf, in the tiny community of Moorhusen, Ostfriesland, Germany on January 22, 1853.

Just a few miles from the moors, the land was more easily drained. Dairy and sheep farming, where almost all the work was done by hand labor, were the primary sources of livelihood. My ancestors provided some of that labor.

My paternal great grandfather, Berend Geerds Janssen Slooter, was born on September 2, 1847 in Wirdum, Germany, nine miles southwest of Moorhusen and away from the moors. His mother, Neeske Jansen Mennenga, was thirty-two years old and his father, Geerd Dirks Lubben Slooter, was age twenty-nine when Berend was born. Geerd worked as a laborer on a farm near Wirdum.

Berend was age twenty-three when he and his brother, Lubbe, were called upon to fight in the Franko-Prussian war of 1870-1871. Lubbe, a musketeer, was killed in battle in September, 1870. Berend, who was in the cavalry and was issued his own horse and saber, survived the war to return home to Wirdum. He met Tatje Wilts and they were married in the thirteenth century Evangelical Reform Church in Wirdum on July 11, 1874. They lived for a short time in Munkeboe, Ostfriesland, Germany, a very small community bordering Moorhusen on the west, before moving to Wirdum where Berend worked as a farm laborer.

Their first child, a daughter, Neeske Berends Slooter, was born in November, 1874. A second girl, Elske Berend Slooter, was born June 1, 1876, and a third girl, Dena Slooter was born September 22, 1878. Their fourth child, a boy (and my grandfather), William Slooter, was born July 13, 1881. On July 28, 1883, two years after the birth of their son, Tatje, my great grandmother, fell ill and died of what was believed to be "nerve fever". She was thirty years old. After remaining a widower for three years, my great grandfather, then age thirty-seven, married Lauke Betten Schipper. They had three children together.

Germany seemed to be in an almost constant state of political turmoil during the late eighteen hundreds as Bismarck, Chancellor of the German state of Prussia, tried to unify Germany. After the Austro-Prussian war of 1866, Hannover, which included Ostfriesland, was annexed by Prussia. A worldwide economic depression, combined with heightened economic and social tensions under the Prussian monarchy, served to make living conditions even less tolerable.

Like most people in Europe at that time, Berend and Lauk were experiencing extremely difficult times. They longed to live where they could own land and eat well, where they could vote and enjoy a sense of equality, and where their children could get an education and realize opportunities denied their parents. The Slooters heard about the high demand for labor and the hope for all those things in America. They caught "America fever" which spread through Europe like a contagious disease in the late nineteenth century. Millions of Europeans were going to America and millions more were talking about going. Berend and Lauk wanted to take their family and go to America!

About that same time, a wealthy American farmer from near Secor, Illinois (about twenty-five miles east of Peoria) traveled to Ostfriesland, Germany, encouraging people to immigrate to America. He met Berend and offered to pay passage for him and his family if Berend would work on one of his farms for a period of time to repay him. To Berend, this sounded like an opportunity and a reasonable deal. He and his family would have a place to live and a living while he was repaying his debt. He accepted the proposition and they made a contract.

Berend, Lauke, and family, now six children, left from Bremen, Germany on a steamship of the **"Norddeutscher Lloyd in Bremen"** line and sailed to America in 1892. On October 27, 1892, Berend went to the courthouse in Eureka, Illinois, and signed a "letter of intent" to become a citizen of The United States of America. At last, they had fulfilled their dream. They were home in America! My grandfather, William, was eleven years old.

Berend's brothers, Jan and Geerd, along with their families, immigrated to America a short time later. The three brothers' first names were changed to Ben, John, and George. Around the year 1900, the second "o" was dropped from the name Slooter to become Sloter. According to my research, all Sloters living in America today are descendents of those three brothers. Even though the Sloter name can be found in Holland, there is no one with the Sloter name living in or around Wirdum, Germany, today!

The characteristics of being self-assured, confident, and adventuresome, and their willingness to take calculated risks, brought my ancestors to America. Those same characteristics have revealed themselves in the generations of the Sloter family that have followed.

THE DREAM

It was near the end of February, 1944, when we started out in our 1935 Ford. The trailer behind was a modified shell of a travel trailer. Dad had cut out a section and moved the roof down to reduce wind resistance and to make it less top-heavy. It was loaded with the bare necessities to set up housekeeping nearly two thousand miles away. We were moving from Kanawha, Iowa to Yakima, Washington!

About a half year earlier, Dad met Herman Rayfield while working at Decker's Meat Packing Plant in Mason City, Iowa. Dad was "pulling leaf lard" and Herman worked on the line nearby. To pull leaf lard from inside the hog's rib cage, a thumb was forced between the layer of lard and the ribs. By using a gripping, twisting, pulling motion, the thin membrane of fat was removed from the carcass. The carcasses hung on an overhead conveyer and moved by at one hundred twenty per hour. Two men working side by side, alternated, each pulling every other one. It required a lot of strength and endurance to keep this up for eight hours, day after day.

Dad was thirty-two years old, and big and strong, so he could handle the work -- but his fingernails couldn't. He came home with white gauze bandages wrapped around his fingers because his fingernails had come off. The pain must have been awful. He hated what he was doing, but kept on working there. He had a family to support and jobs were nearly impossible to find.

Mason City is about forty-five miles northeast of Kanawha, where we lived. It was too far to drive back and forth to work, so Dad roomed in Mason City during the week and came home on the weekends. At first, he stayed with the Rayfields, but later found a room in a boarding house. It was during this time that Herman told Dad about picking fruit in the Yakima Valley in the state of Washington, where he had family. "A family can earn a lot of money if they work hard," he said. The more Dad heard, the better it sounded to him! He had always worked hard, but never seemed to earn enough money to put any away. If our whole family worked together maybe, just maybe, we could earn enough money to save some for a change. Maybe even enough to start farming. A dream was born.

That fall, Dad quit his job at the packing plant and traveled to Washington to check out what he had heard. He worked in the orchards doing whatever needed to be done, learning as he went. His system for getting a job was simple. When asked if he had experience, he answered, "Yes, but I'd like to have you show me how you want it done." When asked about pruning fruit trees the first time, he got a little carried away. He told the man, "When you have pruned as many trees as I have, you can call yourself a pruner!" Still, he got the job.

Dad stayed busy that fall pruning fruit trees and working with irrigation in the orchards. He also scouted out orchards where we might get work picking fruit within a forty-five mile radius of the city of Yakima. Satisfied that our family could do well in that faraway state, and being lonesome for his family, Dad came home in December.

Somehow, Mom managed to keep food on the table and the bills paid while Dad was gone. Even though Mom had four children to care for, and a cow to milk morning and night, she made "homemade" bread and sold it for ten cents a loaf, did house cleaning for eighteen cents an hour and took in washing and ironing for other families in town, earning one dollar a basket.

She took Don and Sandy with her to work while Julian and I were in school. Mom was always there when we got home from school, so we never noticed that she was working outside the home. Julian and I helped as much as we could by doing whatever chores we could handle. The cow had to be fed. We would put a halter and rope on her and tie her to a stake that we drove into the ground where there was grass to graze on along the road ditch. We would stake her out before we went to school, then move her when we got home after school. When the weather was bad, we fed her hay and oat hulls that Dad had stored in the barn that fall.

The barn had to be cleaned. We loaded manure onto a wheelbarrow that I made using scrap lumber and an old steel wheel that I got from the "junk yard". Using a pitchfork, we spread the manure on our large garden north of the house.

We used oat hulls for the cow's bedding, which proved to be almost perfect. It absorbed liquid from the cow droppings better than the oat straw which was normally used. It was easy to scoop up and load on the wheelbarrow, and was easy to spread.

Oat hulls encased the oat grain and were collected when the grain elevator cleaned the oats before the grain was stored and shipped. It was waste that needed to be disposed of, so the elevator manager was happy to give us as much as we needed. We were thankful for the oat hulls because straw tangled together and was difficult for "us kids" to handle.

Fuel was needed for the cook stove. We brought in wood and corncobs from the "cob house" that Dad had filled before he left. It was comforting to have a basket full of wood beside the stove and a couple of "gunny sacks" full of cobs standing along the wall near the stove on a cold winter night. We also carried out the ashes from the stove and spread them on the garden.

Even though money was tight, Mom managed to save a little every week while Dad was gone. The family savings was in a small, clear glass bank shaped like the liberty bell about six inches tall. Mom and Dad kept it hidden in a dresser drawer in their bedroom. They had been saving dimes for a long time and it was nearly full. In preparation for the trip to Washington, and to assess our exact financial situation, they opened the bottom of the bank, shook the dimes out onto the kitchen table and began counting. The coins were arranged in stacks of ten, and the stacks in groups of ten. When they finished counting, there were ten groups of ten stacks. Mom said, "We have one hundred dollars." I could hardly believe it. I exclaimed, "We're rich! We're rich!"

Dad and Mom made the necessary arrangements and closed up the house. It was a sad day when we parted with our nice little Guernsey cow. I felt sorry for Mom when her Singer sewing machine was sold. She had struggled for so long to make the $2.56-a-month payments to pay for it.

Mom and Dad decided that we would start out as soon as they thought the mountain passes would be clear of snow. They were aware of the risk involved with leaving so early in the year, but Dad wanted to be in Yakima Valley and settled when the cherry-picking season started in the spring.

THE TRIP WEST

Our 1935 Ford was running well. Dad had had the 85-horsepower V-8 engine overhauled in preparation for the trip.

But the rest of the car was far from perfect. For one thing, the tires were nearly smooth. It was wartime and tires were almost impossible to get. New tires on the "black market", if you could find them, were very expensive. Buying used tires was Dad's only option. Experience had taught him to look at the carcass of a used tire and not the tread. A used tire with good tread usually had a break in the cotton cords or a "boot" over a break. Dad would pass them up. Even if the carcass looked good, the cords could be starting to rot because of age. Having a tire "blow out" was a very common occurrence in those days.

The brakes were the old mechanical type. This meant that, even at their best, they didn't work very well. Another very obvious thing that was wrong -- the top one-third of the steering wheel was missing. I thought it looked like Dad was flying an airplane. But he must have been used to it, because I never did see him reach for the section that was gone. I wondered about that, however.

Mom and Dad studied the road map and determined that there were two basic routes that we could take. Mom referred to them as "the northern route" and "the southern route". Hoping to avoid bad weather, they chose "the southern route" which would take us through Blair, Nebraska; Cheyenne, Wyoming; Salt Lake City, Utah; Boise, Idaho; Pendleton, Oregon, and then into Washington from the south.

When everything was packed and ready to go, the family piled into the car. There were Mom and Dad, four kids and our dog, Pal. I was nine, Julian, almost eight, Don, five, and Sandy, seven months.

Pal was a large "half chow" that looked a lot like a chow with his long dense coat and blackish tongue. His disposition, however, was a combination of chow and rat terrier. He was smart, alert, and protective of our family, but not vicious. We really loved that dog! He was part of the family. There was never a question as to whether or not he was going with us.

It was snowing when we loaded into the car and left Kanawha early that morning, the last part of February, 1944. My parents had decided earlier when we would leave. Dad was anxious to get going and wasn't about to let a little snow stop us. It was still dark when we pulled out of the driveway, turned onto the gravel road leading south out of Kanawha, and started working our way to Highway 3 about fifteen miles away. It was the closest hard-surface road that would take us to U.S. Highway 30, the "Lincoln Highway". It was the best and most traveled east-west road across America. The 3300-mile *Lincoln Memorial Highway*, named for President Abraham Lincoln, was America's first transcontinental highway and the first federal highway. It stretched across the center of the United States from Times Square in New York City to Lincoln Park in San Francisco, California. Conceived in 1912, that "improved" road was completed in time for the Panama-Pacific Exposition in San Francisco in 1915. It consisted almost entirely of graded dirt and gravel at that time. Taking the path of least resistance, it followed part of the famous Oregon Trail, traveled by pioneers in covered wagons on their way west. By 1925, the entire highway had been paved. Nineteen years later, we would be making use of that narrow ribbon of concrete.

We had just gotten onto Highway 3 when we had our first problem. We were just a little over fifteen miles from home when one of the trailer tires blew out. Dad didn't seem to mind. He just took it in stride and did what had to be done. After removing the wheel and tire, he left us in the car beside the road and, rolling the tire along beside him, started walking the six miles to Clarion. We could still see him when someone picked him up and gave him a ride into town. Locating a good used tire in a strange community proved to be quite a challenge. Dad ended up going to the courthouse to get a permit to buy a tire. It seemed to us that a long time had passed when finally someone stopped his car beside us and Dad got out with a good tire. Soon we were on our way, glad to be moving again.

By the time we reached Denison, Iowa, the snow was coming down a little harder, but Dad kept going. When we drove into the small, western Iowa town of Dunlap about a half-hour later, it was snowing hard and there was about a six or eight-inch accumulation on the streets and highway. This tiny farm community is hilly, with Main Street and the town's only stop sign at the top of a large hill. Dad was forced to stop for traffic about halfway up the hill. When he tried to start out again, the smooth tires wouldn't grip. The car wouldn't move forward, but slid sideways and jackknifed with the trailer into the other side of the highway in the way of oncoming traffic. There was just enough room for a car to get past. There we were, stuck in the middle of the most traveled east-west highway in the nation! Once again, Dad left us in the car and went for help.

5

Cars backed up behind us, and those coming up over the crest of the hill and down toward us were barely able to get by. We worried about what would happen if a big truck would come; it surely wouldn't be able to stop. But we stayed in the car and waited.

After awhile, Dad returned -- alone! He hadn't been able to get any help! When he learned that no help was available, he decided to buy a set of tire chains. Everyone in town was sold out. The only thing he could find was 'emergency' tire chains. They had two cross bars and a strap that fit through a hole in the rim and were buckled to hold them in place. Dad put two chains opposite each other on each rear tire. This left large spaces between the chains. This time when Dad tried to start out, the tires would slip and grab, slip and grab, but the car still didn't move. The trailer was really holding us back. Just then we saw a Greyhound bus come over the hill and it was coming fast! That bus would never be able to miss us or stop on its way down the hill. Dad put the gas pedal to the floor and held it there. The engine roared and the wheels spun, slipping and grabbing, slipping and grabbing and throwing snow. Our hearts pounded while we waited for the crash. Slowly, the car started to move. Just as our car and trailer straightened out and got to the right side of the road, the bus roared by, engulfing us in snow. It had missed us!

By this time, it was late afternoon and would soon be getting dark. We all needed to get out of the car. After reaching level ground, Dad pulled off the highway and parked on a side street to let us get out and stretch our legs. When the back door was opened, Pal suddenly acted like a caged animal with freedom in sight. He was out of the car and running before we knew what was happening. He soon disappeared behind some buildings. We called and called, but he was gone! We ran down the street and into yards until we saw him and called some more, but he would just look at us and run the other way. Why wouldn't he come? He had always come before when we called. But not this time. By now, "us kids" were in tears. We thought for sure that we would have to leave and would never see Pal again. Mom and Dad didn't seem too concerned, but they made an effort to get him to come back, too. I think they understood that he needed to run off some energy and would come back when he was ready. Before long, Pal did come back. We got hold of him and were determined that we would not let him get away again. From then on, the car door was never opened unless someone had hold of our special dog, our Pal.

THE FIRE STATION

It was too late to go on and everyone was tired of being cooped up in the car. There were no hotels or motels in Dunlap, so Dad went to the police station for help in finding a place to stay. There was nothing available. The police told Dad that they wouldn't allow us to leave town because of the weather. It was a real problem; we couldn't stay in the car. As Dad turned to leave the police station, one of the officers said, "Maybe you could stay in the fire station, at least it would be warm." Dad went to the fire station and told the man on duty about our problem and, indeed, he did agree to let us stay there overnight! It was not the best situation, but we had no other choice. There were no cots or beds available, but at least it would be warm and maybe we would be able to get some rest. Don was running a fever again and Mom was worried. She was anxious to take special care of him.

We had all missed Dad when he had gone to Washington, but I think Don missed him the most.

"After Dad came home, Don stuck to him like glue."

Dad was busy making arrangements for the big move and Don wanted to be with him wherever he went. It was cold winter weather and Don ended up getting sick. The doctor said he had double pneumonia. Mom was still nursing him back to health when the day came for us to leave for Washington. Don was feeling much better, but Mom wondered whether we should be going since he wasn't completely well. Mom and Dad checked with the doctor and were told that it should be okay to go. With that, they decided to go ahead as planned. Don still had a slight fever that morning when we left Kanawha.

That night in the fire station, on the back step of one of the fire trucks, Mom gave Don an enema to bring his temperature down. His temperature was near normal the next day. We were all concerned about him and relieved to have him feeling better. It was good to see some of his old sparkle coming back.

After spending a restless night trying to sleep on the running boards and back steps of the fire trucks, Mom fixed us a good breakfast. She brought food along for the trip and cooked it on a camp stove that was always handy in the back of the trailer. "Us kids" thought it was great fun.

The snowplows had worked through the night and the roads were clear. Dad took the emergency tire chains off the wheels, filled the car with gas and we were on our way. By now, everyone was exhausted. We all slept as Dad headed out across Nebraska. Julian and I were on the outside next to the doors and Don in the middle of the back seat. Don leaned against one or the other of us as he slept. Sandy lay on the front seat between Mom and Dad. Mom laid her head on a pillow against the passenger window. Pal took his place on the floor in the back. Mom never did any of the driving on that trip. She was afraid to even try with that trailer behind and the broken steering wheel. The driving was all up to Dad.

Somewhere in the middle of Nebraska, we heard an odd rumbling, pinging sound in the back and the trailer seemed to be leaning to the left. Dad pulled the car and trailer off the road onto the shoulder as far as he could – but a foot or more of the car and trailer was still on the highway. When Dad went back to see what was wrong, he found that all of the steel spokes in one of the trailer wheels had broken. The load had been too much for it. The outer part of the rim was still in place, and the center hub was sitting on it. We had no spare wheel for the trailer. The only thing Dad could do was jack up the trailer, take the wheel off and hitch a ride into the nearest town to see if he could find a wheel. The family once again waited in the car while Dad did what was necessary to get us back on the road.

The road was narrow and the traffic approaching on our side of the highway moved to the left, some vehicles even crossing the center line, in order to miss us as they passed. Even so, the car and trailer rocked in the wind, especially when a truck went by. Time had dragged on each time Dad had left us, but this time was the worst yet. It seemed as though we waited for hours as we watched each truck come toward us, worrying that it would hit us or blow the trailer off the jack. We watched intently as each truck approached us from the direction Dad had gone, hoping and praying that he would be in it.

Watching the rearview mirror, we could see the traffic coming from the east as well as from the west. So, we saw them coming — a semi-truck bearing down on us from the east and another from the west! They appeared to be about the same distance away. Neither slowed down nor sped up. They both just kept coming. The closer they got, the more sure we were that they would meet right where we were sitting. There wasn't room for all of us -- there just wasn't room! We sat and waited as they came closer and closer. We held our breath and waited. Then they were upon us. As we had feared, they met right where we were -- and roared by. There was no crash, no scraping -- just the roar of the trucks and the car rocking in the wind. Miraculously, they had missed us -- and the trailer had stayed on the jack! We all gave a big sigh of relief. But then, we couldn't help but wonder -- would it happen again? And, if it did, would they miss us again?

Finally, a truck pulled up and stopped. Dad got out carrying an odd-looking wheel and tire -- the only thing he had been able to find in that little town that would fit. It was an implement wheel from some type of farm machinery. Dad said it was stronger than the spoke-wheel that broke. He put it on the trailer, let the jack down, and we were on our way again, thankful to be rolling down the road in one piece!

Fire truck we slept in and on in the Dunlap fire station.

9

NIGHT DRIVING

It was late at night when we parked near the front door of an old, rundown motel in Cheyenne, Wyoming. The trip across Nebraska had seemed endless.

After Dad got the broken trailer wheel changed somewhere in Nebraska, we traveled the remainder of the day and into the night without incident. We enjoyed the changing scenery for a while, but eventually it seemed that things didn't change much. Mom traded seats with "us kids" so we could each sit in the front for a while. She entertained us by telling stories about when she was a little girl, singing songs to us and reading to us when we weren't napping. We especially enjoyed having her read "The Pony Rider Boys" which she rationed out, reading one chapter at a time. Our favorite song was about the cowboy who wanted to go "see his mother when the work was all done in the fall."

Somewhere on the long road across Nebraska, Dad had made a decision. He didn't discuss it with Mom or anyone else, he just decided on his own. The troubles we had experienced so far on this trip had gotten us off to a slow start. Also, Dad's frustration was compounded by the 35-mile-per-hour wartime speed limit. He thought we should have been a lot further down the road by then. We needed to make up some time. He would drive through the night! After working hard to get ready for the trip, then dealing with a flat tire, bad weather, a broken wheel and a sleepless first night out, Dad was going to drive all night!

So, Dad drove! While the rest of us slept, talked, listened to stories, and slept some more, Dad drove. He was like a machine as he drove on and on. Even so, I was sure he had to be getting tired. How could he possibly keep driving? I expected him to fall asleep at any time. On the one hand, I had total confidence in Dad's driving -- to me there wasn't a better driver in the world -- but, on the other hand, I wondered how he could possibly stay awake.

Finally, somewhere in Nebraska, Dad pulled off the road by a service station and laid his head back on his seat to sleep for a while. I was resting in the back seat behind Dad, but not asleep. Suddenly, Dad rose up in his seat and started the car. He didn't say anything, just stared straight ahead like he was in a trance and started the car! He certainly hadn't slept long enough to do any good. Then I knew, I figured it out -- he was sleeping! He was starting the car in his sleep. I reached up, grabbed his shoulders with both hands, shook him as hard as I could and shouted, "Dad, Dad, wake up! You're dreaming -- wake up!" It was late at night and getting cold. Dad had simply started the car to warm up. When the car was warm, he turned the engine off and we all slept a while. I was half-awake when Dad started the car the next time and pulled onto the highway but, this time, I knew things were okay.

There was something special about driving late at night. In those days, highways went through the center of almost all cities and small towns. With the heavy daytime traffic and endless stoplights, it took a long time to get through them. There was almost no traffic at night and the traffic lights were usually just blinking. We could drive through in a fraction of the time. We were in our own quiet little world as we headed west through the night.

As the sun came up behind us, we began to stir in the back seat. It looked as if it was going to be a beautiful day. We were hungry. Mom got us some milk and cereal for breakfast. Sometimes we had fruit. We never had a regular "sit-down" meal on the trip. We got by mostly on sandwiches and snacks. One of Dad's favorite traveling "meals" was a "ring of gut" (bologna) and soda crackers. We could eat that while moving down the road. We would each break a chunk off the ring and pass it on to the next person. Then the cracker box would be passed. We took turns drinking water from a jug. By the time the ring of bologna was gone, we were all satisfied.

Dad must have finally been wearing down. When we stopped for gas and to use the restroom, I watched Dad go across the street. I was still the only one in the car when he came back, and I saw him tuck a bottle of whiskey down in the seat, between the cushion and the backrest. He must have thought that it would help him stay awake. Realizing that I had seen what he had, Dad looked back at me and said, "Don't say anything to Mom, okay?"

Now what? I didn't know what to do. Mom had talked about the problems that drinking alcohol could cause, so I knew it wasn't good -- especially when driving. If I told Mom, Dad would be angry with me and I would feel like I had betrayed him. If I didn't say anything and something bad happened, I would feel responsible. When Mom came back to the car and got in the front seat, the top of the bottle must have been sticking up a little, because she saw it right away. She grabbed it and let Dad know in no uncertain terms that there would be "no drinking" on the trip. I'm sure Dad knew that he was wrong, because he got a sheepish look on his face and didn't answer. I was really glad that I didn't have to make the decision of whether or not to tell Mom.

Mom sent Dad into the station for coffee and we were on our way again. Mom and Dad wanted to reach Cheyenne, Wyoming, and stop for the night. It was dark when we got there. Dad stopped at several motels before finding one that fit our needs -- somewhat. We needed room for everyone to sleep, it had to be clean, we wanted our dog with us and it had to be inexpensive. What we found wasn't too clean, and we had to sneak Pal in, but it had enough room -- and it was cheap. It didn't take us long after the car stopped to unload and get into bed. It felt good to lie down flat and not be moving.

THE MOUNTAINS

It was a novel idea and it worked. We were at six thousand feet elevation in Cheyenne, Wyoming, in February. It was cold outside and the car heater wasn't working very well. How could the car be warmed up without wasting precious gas? Dad got the Coleman camp stove out of the trailer, set it on the ground and lit it. After the stove warmed up and was burning with a nice blue flame, he propped it level in the back seat of the car. By the time we had breakfast in the motel room and were ready to leave, we had a nice warm car waiting for us with the frost melted from the windows.

Heading west into the foothills, we could see the Rocky Mountains in the distance. They looked like a giant wall ahead with no possible way through. Julian and I were excited about crossing the mountains – but Mom wasn't! In fact, she was quite concerned about it. Maybe she worried that Dad would have trouble steering around all the curves with one third of the steering wheel missing. Or maybe she knew that the brakes on the car weren't the best -- or that the old Ford might have trouble pulling the trailer up the steep slopes. Maybe she knew these things, but we didn't -- so we had complete confidence in the car and in Dad's driving. We weren't at all concerned. When Mom began to express her fear, Julian and I made light of it and teased her. Whenever she would say anything about the mountains, we would tell her that they were just "mole hills". She took our teasing fairly well, but we could tell that she was truly concerned. The roads were narrow and curvy and there were some very steep grades.

As we progressed up the mountain and around the curves, things seemed to be going quite well. Then, going down one steep grade, we heard a noise and felt a sudden jerking on the back of the car. All of a sudden, the car was being jerked from side to side like a wild bronco was trying to break loose from it. Something was trying to break loose, all right. It was the trailer! Somehow, Dad managed to keep control and ease the car off to the side of the road. The trailer hitch had broken away from the car bumper, causing the heavily-loaded trailer to "sunfish" violently from side to side, jerking on the safety chains still fastened to the bumper.

It had to be repaired. Mom and Dad really didn't want to leave the trailer on the highway unattended, but there was no choice. Dad blocked the wheels on the trailer and unhooked the safety chains. He disconnected the broken hitch from the trailer tongue and drove to the

13

nearest town to find a welding shop. The man in the welding shop repaired the old hitch and added a steel rod. By wrapping the steel rod around the bumper and the hitch, he made the hitch much stronger than it was before.

As we backtracked up the road, we wondered if the trailer would still be where we had left it and if our possessions would all be there. Everything was there. No one had bothered the trailer or its contents. I helped Dad get the trailer on the hitch and we were soon on the road again, confident that there would be no more hitch problems.

After Cheyenne, the trip took on a whole new feeling. It was no longer necessary for Mom to entertain us. The mountains were so awe-inspiring, the scenery so spectacular, and the mountain roads so curvy, that we were simply captivated by it all.

Mom never got over her fear of mountain driving and we stopped teasing her. Sometimes when we were on a narrow road with a drop-off down to a river hundreds of feet below, we understood her fear. There were times when I silently wished that the steering wheel on the car was all there and that we didn't have a trailer behind. Anything could happen and we didn't need a handicap. But Dad maneuvered the car and trailer skillfully as we traveled up and down the mountain grades and the around curves.

The dangers of mountain driving were made vividly clear to us as we rounded one mountain curve and saw a "trailer house" overturned and on fire by the side of the road. Dad stopped to help and almost had the fire out when the owner came up to him and said, "It's too far gone, just let it burn." That didn't seem right to us at the time, but it was probably the best, and safest, thing to do.

Mom was the navigator and a pretty good one, but once in a while she would make a mistake or, should I say, an "error in judgment". Somewhere in Idaho, Mom studied the map and found a "short cut". By taking Highway 6, we would need to drive just twenty miles instead of the fifty miles it would take to travel "the long way". Mom, who was "scared to death" of mountain driving, chose to take a road that was wildly steep and curving! The map didn't show the sharp curves and precipitous drops, so it appeared to her to be the reasonable thing to do. She was used to the roads in Iowa where mountains and mountain roads don't exist. Once we started on that road with the trailer behind, there was no turning back! The going was very slow -- ten to fifteen miles per hour, at times -- and it taxed our little Ford to the limit. But we made it! As you might imagine, there were no more short cuts on that trip.

14

OUT WEST

There were historical markers and other sites of special interest "Out West" that we often stopped to see. This helped keep us kids from getting too restless in the back seat. Those stops often served more than one purpose. We could stretch our legs and eat a little -- while, at the same time, we were learning about nature and the history of our country. One of our first "point of interest" stops was at Sherman Hill, Wyoming, between Cheyenne and Laramie. First seen by tourists from a train before there were roads, we saw a tree growing out of a large rock. That attraction is still there, but now it is in the median of Interstate 80.

Another attraction and pastime was reading the advertising signs along the way. We especially liked to read the "Burma Shave" signs with their catchy little verses advertising Burma Shave Shaving Cream. A few that come to mind are: "Within this vale of toil and sin, your head grows bald, but not your chin. Burma Shave." "She kissed the hairbrush by mistake, she thought it was her husband, Jake. Burma Shave." "Though tough and rough from wind and wave, your cheek grows sleek with Burma Shave." There were many times, when driving on the two-lane roads after dark, that the driver in an oncoming car wouldn't dim his lights. Dad would always make an unkind comment, so I suppose it was only natural for us to especially enjoy and remember a Burma Shave verse that we read on later trips between Iowa and Washington -- "The famous last words of lights that shine, if he won't dim his, I won't dim mine. Burma Shave."

The broken trailer hitch in Wyoming marked a turning point on our trip west. It was our last car trouble. From then on, we made only planned stops for gas, food and lodging. The motels we stopped at still seemed to justify lifting bed mattresses and holding a lighted match under the springs to check for bedbugs. Sometimes there was only one bed and we would lie crossways, side by side, happy to be able to stretch out for awhile. We never spent much time in bed, however. Dad would drive late into the night and was ready to get going again at daybreak. He continued using the Coleman stove every morning to heat up the interior of the car so it would be warm for us.

Finally, having crossed parts of Iowa, Nebraska, Wyoming, Utah, Idaho, and Oregon, we entered the state of Washington from the south, near Kennewick, where the Yakima River enters the Columbia River on its way to the Pacific Ocean. A couple hours later, Dad said, "That's it folks, that's the Yakima Valley. Isn't it beautiful?" We looked ahead and saw a patchwork of trees in rows, filling the valley below and up the hillsides interspersed with desert landscape. We had to agree. It was a beautiful sight -- in more ways than one. Most importantly, we had made it. We had reached our destination!

That trip was, in many ways, an education in itself. We learned firsthand about such things as -- what mountains are really like, about being above the "tree line" where you see permanent snow fences because it can snow anytime, what continental divides and mountain passes are and how they can be one and the same. We experienced the beauty and sound of clear mountain streams, the smell of fresh mountain air and the scent of the pine forests. We learned about the "Oregon Trail" and saw the tracks where settlers' wagons had gone nearly one hundred years before. We learned that the pursuit of a dream may not be easy and that a shortcut isn't necessarily shorter. We learned about the joy of travel and the thrill of anticipating what lies ahead. These things became a part of us and who we are.

A YOUNG MAN

Near Buffalo Center, Iowa -- 1924

Bill Sloter was a rangy, rawboned kid – and very strong for his age. The sixth of fourteen children born to William and Anna Sloter, Bill was given heavy work to do on the family farm when he was still a young boy. It seemed to him that he was required to do much more than his share. He reminisced later that the older boys in the family, Earl and Ben, were very good at "getting out of work". For recreation, as he was growing up, Bill often competed in feats of strength and wrestled with "the Hendrichs boys" who lived on a neighboring farm. He competed with the older boys in that family on an equal basis, beating them as often as not.

Bill's grandparents had emigrated from Germany to America in 1892 when Bill's father, William, was eleven years old. They settled near Eureka, Illinois, where Bill's grandfather worked on a farm to pay for the family's passage to America. William grew up near Eureka where he met and fell in love with a young woman whose parents had also immigrated to America from Germany. Anna Johnson was born in Eureka, Illinois, in 1881. William was twenty-six and Anna was twenty-four when they were married in 1905. They moved to Tea, South Dakota, where they started farming. The couple used Anna's five-thousand-dollar dowry (a large amount of money in 1905) to finance their venture. William had experience with beef cattle and, although he knew that there was risk involved, he convinced Anna that they should use part of their money to add feeding beef cattle to their regular farming operation. The risk in "cattle feeding" came in the cost of feeder cattle compared to the market price of "fat cattle", as well as the cost of feed and the possibility of cattle dying, or "death loss".

William and Anna started their family right away. A baby boy was born and they named him Earl. When he was just a few months old, Earl got sick and died. William and Anna were devastated. Before long, however, Anna told William that she was pregnant again. Another boy was born and they named him Earl, also, in honor of the son they had lost. Their family continued to grow. Next came Bertha, then Anna, Ben, Bill (on February 5, 1911 in Tea, South Dakota), Louis, Esther, Kathryn, Edmund, Clarence, Ethel and Francis. Another boy died in infancy along the way.

Their venture into "the cattle business" proved to be disastrous. The price of fat cattle dropped "out of sight" and soon the five-thousand-dollar dowry was gone. Totally discouraged, they left their farm in South Dakota and moved to Buffalo Center, Iowa, and started over.

From as far back as Bill could remember, until leaving home, he heard about the five thousand dollars that his father had lost in the cattle business. Anna would never let her husband forget it and brought it up whenever they had an argument.

William and Anna were very strict with their children and were harsh disciplinarians. Punishment for "getting out of line" was often excessive. Bill frequently thought about how he would like to get away from the arguing, severe punishment and hard work.

One day while working together in the barn, Bill and his father got into an argument. When his father took a swing at him, Bill instinctively sidestepped, grabbed his dad's arm and pulled him off balance. His father tried to catch himself as he fell and ended up with a broken thumb. William picked himself up, looked at his thirteen-year-old son, Bill, and said, "It looks like you're getting too big for me to handle anymore." He left the barn and went to the house. The fracas ended, but the tension between Bill and his father remained. Bill's relationship with his mother, a very strong-willed, domineering woman, wasn't much better.

Soon after the incident in the barn, Bill decided it was time for him to leave. Just before dawn one morning, he quietly opened his second-story bedroom window and threw a bag containing a few clothes to the ground. He climbed out, hung from the windowsill for a moment, then dropped to the ground. Bill picked up the bag, waved good-bye to his sister, Bertha, who was watching him, and walked away. He never looked back. At age thirteen, with a fourth-grade education, Bill Sloter was on his own!

William Sloter
(Grandpa)

Anna (Johnson) Sloter
(Grandma)

SURVIVAL

Life didn't get any easier for Bill after he left home. On the day that he left, he walked about five miles to his Uncle Lloyd's farm where he knew they were looking for help. Bill hired out for room and board and a small amount of money each month.

Things went reasonably well for a while. Bill was expected to do the work of a man, and he did. But he often felt that he was being treated like a boy. Room and board came naturally, but the pay didn't. When payday would come around, he would either be shorted or, sometimes, not paid at all. Bill's uncle would give a variety of reasons and excuses. To make matters worse, soon after he left home, Bill's father left his mother. Anna knew where Bill was working and came to see him, insisting that he give her money to help support the family. Although Bill had very little money, he gave his mother what he could. And, over time, he continued to help support the family from wherever he was. Since getting paid what he was owed seemed hopeless, one morning Bill gathered up his belongings and left. His uncle, Lloyd, protested, but Bill just walked out the door and kept going.

Over the next few years, Bill had several different jobs as "hired man on the farm", all of which he eventually left for one reason or another. For example, one farmer sent him outside to rub his car while it was raining so the rainwater could rinse it clean. Bill was still being treated like a boy!

In those days, after a week's work on the farm, it was customary to "go to town" on Saturday night to buy groceries and supplies for the next week and to socialize with friends and neighbors. One Saturday night, there was a carnival in town and they were advertising for help. Bill saw an opportunity for adventure, a chance to get away from the situation he was in and from the burden his mother was placing on him. By this time, the youngest of his sisters had been "adopted out" so the needs of the family had changed. His mother should now be able to get by on her own. With a clear conscience, Bill joined the carnival and left town. He was sixteen years old.

Working as a roustabout, Bill learned the inside workings of carnival life. Some of it was good and some not so good, such as how to take unfair advantage of someone if the opportunity presented itself.

While working and being exposed to the day-to-day routine of carnival life, Bill enjoyed listening to the lyrical "carnival calls" at the various attractions. Eventually he got to know them by heart. This enabled him to occasionally work as a "barker" when someone needed time off. He liked the change of pace.

Traveling with the carnival was a relatively carefree time for Bill and he enjoyed the excitement of it all. But that life ended for him with the arrival of the "Great Depression" following the stock market crash of 1929. The carnival shut down.

Jobs were not just hard to find, there were simply no jobs available! Joining the ranks of the thousands of men of all ages and all walks of life who were unemployed, Bill went "on the bum". He was just eighteen years old when he got acquainted with life "on the road". Bill worked for food or sometimes a chicken or vegetables such as cabbage, onions, carrots, potatoes, etc. -- that he would share with his comrades "in camp". The various items brought in by him and others would be thrown into a large pot of water boiling over an open fire. The resulting "mulligan stew" was shared with and enjoyed by all in camp, regardless of whether or not they had been able to furnish anything for the pot. After eating, the men would often talk well into the night, sharing stories about themselves and their experiences.

It was rare for anyone to be able to generate cash, but Bill met a man who seemed to always come up with a little. He was a barber. Carrying a hand clipper, comb and scissors with him at all times, and charging very little, he could usually find someone who would let him cut his hair. He was a small man and probably felt safe with Bill around. He and Bill became friends and traveling companions.

Sleeping in empty railroad boxcars on straw and newspaper, or in "hobo camps" under makeshift shelters, left a lot to be desired. But the objective was survival. By now, Bill stood six-feet-two inches tall and weighed one hundred eighty pounds, toughened by what life had dealt him and educated by "the school of hard knocks". Bill was a survivor.

Thievery among the "men of the road" was common. Wearing your clothes when you slept was the only way to be sure that you would still have them when you woke up -- and sometimes even that didn't work. One morning, Bill woke up in a side-railed boxcar where he had spent the night with some other men and discovered that his shoes were gone. He had been wearing them when he went to sleep. Looking around, he saw a man nearby wearing his shoes. Bill stripped his shoes off the man, grabbed him and threw him out of the boxcar onto the ground. The message was clear and soon got around. Don't mess with "big Bill Sloter".

Another time, something happened in Minneapolis, Minnesota, that caused the police to round up all the "bums" in the city and bring them in for questioning. Bill was among them. As he walked toward the police station with the group of men, one of the policemen poked him in the back several times with the end of his nightstick. Bill stopped and turned around. Looking the policeman straight in the eye, and pointing his finger at his nose, he said, "Poke me with that stick again and I'll knock you on your ass." It didn't happen again.

Bill was a fun-loving guy with a good (some might say crude) sense of humor and an easy laugh. But the sharpened instincts of self-preservation that he developed on the way to becoming a man remained with him throughout his life. His quick, and sometimes violent, reaction when he felt threatened, belittled or insulted, became a permanent part of his make-up. He was a "rough and ready" man among men.

As times improved, Bill returned to what he knew best – farm work. He and his younger brother, Louis, were hitchhiking around in the summer of 1931 looking for work, when they stopped in Britt, Iowa. It just so happened that Billy Smith, who had a farm nine miles southwest of Britt, was in town at the same time looking for help. Somehow, the three men got together. However, Billy had work for only one man. After talking the situation over, Louie and Bill decided that Bill would take the job and Louie would go on. That proved to be a fortuitous decision for Bill. The widow Minnie Jackson, her son, James, and her six daughters were farming the place across the road from the Smiths.

WIDOWED, BUT NOT ALONE

Ackley, Iowa -- 1885

Minnie Brandt was born in Ackley, Iowa on August 26, 1885. Her parents, Carl and Caroline Brand, and their family moved to a farm near Kanawha, Iowa, when she was a very young girl. The family farmed in that area and she was educated in a nearby country school. Minnie grew to womanhood living and working on the farm with her parents. In 1906, she met a nice-looking, mild-mannered young man named Albert Jackson and fell in love. He often wore a hat tipped back on his head, exposing dark, wavy red hair that he parted in the middle. Albert Jackson and Minnie Brandt were married on February 17, 1907. He was twenty-four years of age and she was twenty-two.

Albert and Minnie rented a small farm, on a sharecrop basis, a few miles southeast of Kanawha, not far from where her parents lived. (Sharecropping is where a farmer farms land that he doesn't own and gives the landlord a percentage [usually fifty percent] of the harvested crops as rent.) They started their family and life was good. As the years passed, they established a well-rounded farming operation and their family increased. Eventually, they rented a larger farm -- 160 acres -- three miles west of Kanawha and moved. By that time, Albert and Minnie had increased their livestock on the farm to twelve horses, eighteen cows, a few calves, a flock of nearly two hundred chickens and some hogs.

By the time they had been married nineteen years, Minnie had given birth to nine children. There were James, Caroline, Mary, the twins -- Lela and Lula, Gladys, and Alma. Carl and Mabel had both died at an early age. On February 25, 1926 another, and "unexpected", member was added to the family. Caroline was only sixteen when her son was born out of wedlock. It was a shock to her family and devastating to her father. But Caroline's son, Clarence, soon became an accepted part of the family. No one seemed to know why, but he became "Bobby", and later, "Bob".

Albert supplemented the farm income by contracting with Hancock County to grade a few miles of road for $80 per month. That job amounted to pulling a "king drag" up and down the road with one of their teams of horses, to fill in wheel ruts created when the dirt or

23

thinly-graveled roads turned to mud with the spring rains. A king drag was simply two wooden "bridge planks", three inches by twelve inches by about ten feet long, positioned on edge about two feet apart and fastened together. A platform to hold rocks for ballast was built on top of the planks. Rocks were added or removed depending on the depth of the ruts to be filled. A chain fastened near the ends of one of the planks provided the means to hitch up a team of horses. The drag pulled hard and provided a good workout for the horses.

Albert went to Kanawha almost every day to deliver cream from their dairy herd to the creamery and bring back buttermilk for their hogs. He also sold butter, which had been churned by the children, to the J.O. Johnson Store. "God, how I hated that churn! But as I look back, those were the good old days," said their daughter, Mary, at age eighty-four.

Albert regularly remembered his children with a little treat from town. He always made them feel special, especially the twins. They loved him dearly.

In the summer of 1926, Albert rented a different farm and began making preparations to move the family in the spring of 1927. He was excited about the "new" 240-acre farm centered between the towns of Kanawha, Corwith and Britt in Hancock County, Iowa. It was some of the flattest, most fertile farmland in the world. Albert, his son, James, and Bill Meyer, a farm hand, went to the new farm in the fall of 1926 and did "fall plowing" on all of the crop land. It was ready to be worked-up and planted in the spring.

Although Albert was a strong man, he was plagued with many ailments. Sadly, he died on October 7, 1926, at the age of forty-three, leaving Minnie alone with seven children to feed, clothe and raise. There was no life insurance. It was not common to carry insurance on one's life in those days.

After Albert's untimely death, Minnie considered her situation and what to do about earning a living and raising her children. She would be receiving a government "widow's pension" of eight dollars per month for each child under age eighteen. That would help, but it wouldn't go far. It would take a lot more money than that for them to live and she wasn't sure she could find a job that would pay enough for her to support her family. If she did find a job, where would they live -- and who would take care of her children? The idea of putting the children up for adoption was unthinkable. It wasn't even considered. But there were certainly more questions than answers.

Newlyweds Albert Jackson and Minnie (Brand) Jackson

THE NEW FARM

February, 1927

If she could keep the farm, maybe she and her family could do the work. Minnie and her husband had always made decisions together concerning the farm operation, so she thoroughly understood the business of farming. The machinery she owned was "antique" but in good condition, so she could probably get by with what she had. When farming, if you have livestock for meat, eggs and milk, and a big garden for vegetables, there is always plenty to eat. Minnie had plenty of livestock and the family could raise a big garden. If they could stay "on the farm", food for the family would not be a problem.

Buildings for livestock, and a home, are part of the benefits of being a tenant farmer -- so if they could stay on the farm, they would also have a place to live. And she would be there to care for her own children. After considering all the "pros and cons", Minnie decided that the best thing for her family would be for her to continue farming. But with Albert gone, she wasn't sure that their new landlord would allow her to farm his land without a man. After considerable discussion with George Oxley, the landowner's farm manager, Minnie was able to convince him that, with her experience and her children to help, she could do a good job of farming the land and raise good crops.

Doing a good job was of utmost importance, because with a sharecrop agreement the landlord receives a percentage of the harvested crops as rent. Consequently, the ability of a tenant farmer and the yield of the crops he raises directly affect how much rent the landlord receives at the end of the year. Their sharecrop agreement was 50/50. Fifty percent of the harvested crops would go to the landlord and fifty percent to the tenant. The crops would be divided as they were harvested by putting one load into the landlord's storage and one into the tenant storage, alternating as they worked their way across the field. The landlord would eventually sell his share, attempting to time his sale to get the best price. But the tenant would feed most of his share to his livestock, expecting to end up with more money when the milk, eggs and livestock were sold than could be realized by just selling the grain. It was a lot more work marketing crops "through livestock", but it generally paid off in the end.

When changing farms, the first of March is the traditional moving day. On March 1, 1927, Minnie and her children, with the help of their "hired man", Bill Meyer, moved house furnishings, machinery, grain, hay, straw bedding and livestock to their new "place" -- and a new life.

The house was big and drafty with no curtains at the windows. The girls thought it was "spooky" at first and always felt that someone might be looking in at them at night. They didn't like it. The farm was not set up for dairy farming. The barn had enough stalls for her horses, but only had stanchions enough for ten cows. Their eighteen cows were an important part of the farm operation and Minnie was determined to keep them all. She decided to use the alleyway of the corncrib and a "box stall" in the barn to house the additional cows. Doing the chores morning and night, with the cows scattered out in the different locations around the farm, would be awkward, but it would work.

Not only was their new farm a good farm with rich soil and flat fields, but it was also well located. Corwith was only five miles away and Kanawha seven miles. That was important, because Minnie didn't know how to drive a car. When she had tried to learn, soon after Albert died, she narrowly missed backing over her daughter, Alma, who was playing in the farmyard. Alma wasn't hurt, but it so frightened Minnie that she never got in the driver's seat again.

They did have an old car, though -- an old Buick -- that James or Caroline would occasionally drive. The roads were mostly ungraded dirt paths laid out across the prairie, with weeds and grass growing in the fencerows along both sides, and thinly-graveled graded roads. If there was any snow at all, many of the roads would drift full with up to fifteen-foot drifts. Snow was not removed from the roads, so it would be packed down by whatever traffic that got through. The surest way to know you would get where you wanted to go, and back home again, was to hitch a team to a bobsled or buggy. If there was much snow at all, it was often easier to cut the fences and go through the fields "cross country" than to try to go by road. So the car was seldom driven.

The Jacksons took weekly trips to town to sell eggs and occasionally a few chickens to buy supplies. Sometimes they went to Corwith, but they preferred doing business at the J.O. Johnson Store in Kanawha where they could both sell their produce and buy what they needed. If they needed a small item or two during the week, they would usually go by horseback to the "Stilson General Store" two miles north of their farm instead of going all the way to town.

27

A FARM FAMILY

Work on the farm, both around the house and outside, was divided among the children according to their age and ability. Housework included baking bread, preparing meals and washing clothes for nine people. It also included cleaning house, carrying in wood or corn cobs to burn in the stoves, hauling out ashes, carrying in water to fill the cook-stove reservoir (which was their source of hot water), caring for the smaller children and miscellaneous chores.

Outside, there were cows to milk, milk separating to do, and eggs to "pick"; chickens, hogs and cows to feed; chicken house, hog house, and cow and horse barns to clean, and manure to "pitch" into the spreader and spread on the fields. Field work included plowing, disking and dragging the fields to prepare them for planting, as well as planting the "row crops" and seeding oats. After the row crops were up, they needed to be cultivated to keep the weeds down. The oat crop was cut and bundled in the summer. The bundles needed to be stacked in shocks (shocking oats) to keep the grain dry and prevent spoilage until "thrashing time". The older members of the family worked at that hot, backbreaking job. Thrashing the oats followed, which also involved the whole family in one way or another. Then came the corn harvest season in the fall, and the "big push" to get the corn picked (by hand) and into the crib before bad weather set in. Extra "hands" were hired for corn harvest. The Jacksons also raised a big garden which needed tending. Firewood was cut with a two-man saw and stacked during the winter months and allowed to dry or "season" for one or two years before it was ready to burn in the stoves. There was always plenty to do on the farm. Everyone in the family that was old enough to work "pitched in" and did their part to get the work done.

The Jackson children were introduced to work and given responsibility almost as soon as they could walk. Their first work experience usually centered on the chicken flock. The younger children would help the older ones feed and water the baby chicks or gather eggs. Eventually, as they grew older, the children were made responsible for other small tasks and were expected to work on their own. And they were expected to do the job right. If they broke an egg, for example, the discipline was severe enough that they never wanted it to happen again.

As the children grew, they learned to appreciate the value of hard work and of being responsible. Eventually they were allowed to adopt an "old cluck" (setting hen) and raise a brood of chicks and later raise a "club calf" for a 4H Club project. Profit from the eventual sale of their animals was theirs to keep.

Minnie made the final decisions on the farm, but James, the eldest (age nineteen), was given the responsibility of overseeing the outside work, including the chores and getting the field work done. That first year on the new farm, Caroline (seventeen), Mary (fourteen), Lela and Lula (twelve), and Gladys (seven), were each expected to do chores and work in the fields, and they did. Minnie made sure of that. Alma was only two and Bobby one, so the older girls were basically responsible for caring for them, as well. Eventually, Minnie even rented an additional eighty acres across the road, so the family had a total of 320 acres to farm. That was a lot of land to farm with horse-drawn equipment.

Minnie was a strong woman and a strong disciplinarian. She was in control and sometimes maintained that control by using a razor strap on the backs of her children.

"If one of the other kids was 'getting it', you had better not laugh! If you did, you could get it worse. More than once, we went upstairs to a bedroom and counted each other's welts".

The Jackson children didn't like the harsh discipline, but they loved their mother and took their punishment in stride.

There was little doubt, the family would make it.

SCHOOL DAYS

Country roads are laid out in one-mile grids on the plains of Iowa. During the 1930's and 1940's, there was a country school every two miles, serving four square miles or "sections". So, theoretically, no child would need to walk more than two miles to school. But sometimes, when the weather was bad, that mile or two seemed terribly long. No matter what the weather, the children would either walk to school or ride a pony. Even at twenty degrees below zero, the children were expected to be in school. There was no begging off. On cold days, the teacher would arrive at school early enough to get a fire going in the heating stove, which was located in the middle of the room, so the room would be warm by the time the students arrived. The "big boys" would help by bringing in firewood for the stove during the day.

After moving, Lela, Lula, and Gladys finished the school year in the one-room country school located just across the corner from their farm. They graduated from the eighth grade there, Lela and Lula in 1928 and Gladys in 1933. Being convinced that it was important to have a high school education, they decided to continue on and to graduate from high school. Lela, Lula, and Gladys were the only children in the family who went beyond the eighth grade.

Lela and Lula attended ninth grade at Kanawha High School. Since it was too far to travel back and forth morning and night, they would normally stay in town with their uncle, Louis Jackson, and his family. Their older brother, James, would hitch a team of horses to a bobsled (a farm wagon with runners in place of wheels) and take them the seven miles to Kanawha on Monday morning, arriving in time for school, and would pick them up after school on Friday. During the long rides to and from town, the girls would huddle down in the back of the box, out of the wind, and would cover themselves with an old blanket in an effort to keep warm. Oat straw scattered in the box helped to cushion the ride somewhat.

At Uncle Louis' place, the twins were given a room in which to sleep and had access to the cook stove, but that was all. The twelve-year-old girls would bring their own, very limited groceries from home and cook their own meals. They certainly didn't live "high on the hog". Their meals consisted mostly of corn meal mush for breakfast, bread and jelly sandwiches for school lunch, and potatoes and onions for supper. After cooking their meal on the cook stove in the kitchen, they would carry it to their upstairs bedroom to eat while

30

sitting on the side of the bed. Humble as the food was, their cousins would often ask if they could have some. Times were hard. It seemed as if no one had any money.

After finishing ninth grade in Kanawha, Lela and Lula transferred to Corwith High School. It was two miles closer to the farm and they could ride the "horse bus". The five miles to high school in Corwith didn't seem far when the weather was good. But it seemed like a very long way when the weather was bad. Also, since the horse bus didn't go past their place, the girls had to walk a mile on an ungraded dirt road to board it. The horse bus looked much like a small motor-powered bus, but was pulled by two horses. There was no heat. Sometimes when the bus was late, they would have to stand in the cold and wait for it. If it took too long, they could go to Oxley's farmhouse nearby to warm up.

When it snowed, the path to the bus would usually drift full. If the girls were forced to wade through the snow, it would collect in their stockings, melt, and soak into their long underwear and freeze. There was no heat on the bus and no way to warm up on the way to school. They would often walk to the bus with Terry Long, a kind and thoughtful neighbor boy. He would walk ahead of them so they could follow in his footsteps. This would help keep their stockings and long underwear dry for a more comfortable ride to school.

Farm chores had to be done before school and each member of the family was assigned a task. The twins, Lela and Lula, would take turns between "outside chores" and "inside chores". One week, one of the twins would milk three cows that were in a box stall in the barn while the other would bake bread, fix school lunches and cook breakfast for everyone -- then the next week they would switch responsibilities.

Milking was one of the girls' "least favorite" jobs. Sitting on a one-legged stool, they would lean their head against the cow's side to help keep their balance while cradling the milk pail between their knees. The cow's hair, where the girls leaned their head, was often caked with manure. And there was always the threat of the cow kicking, sending the milker, pail and stool flying. They used hobbles on the legs of known "kickers", but still got surprised once in a while.

A strong person with experience could milk a cow by hand in a relatively short time, making the milk foam up as it was squirted into the pail. But the young girls were neither experienced milkers, nor very strong. Their arms and hands would get very tired as they took a cow's teat in each hand and alternately squeezed, first gripping with the index finger, then with the middle fingers and finally the

31

little finger, while pulling down on the teat at the same time. Each stroke would yield about one-fourth cup of milk and each cow gave between three and four gallons. It took them a long time to milk those three cows. The girls felt proud if they could get the milk to foam up a little in the pail. The twins' outside chores were finished when the cows were milked, the milk carried to the barn and poured into milk cans, the manure cleaned from the stall and new bedding put down, and the cows watered and fed.

On cold winter mornings, the morning inside chores included lighting fires in the heating stove and the cook stove to warm the house. The cook stove needed to be hot and ready for cooking breakfast, no matter what the weather. Lela and Lula were often the first ones up and both working at getting the fires going before one of them would go outside to "do chores". The whole family, except the small children, was always up early to get the chores done and breakfast over so the girls could change clothes and clean themselves up before going to school.

"More than once, when we didn't have time to really get cleaned up, we went to school with cow shit under our fingernails."

Once, while riding toward home on the "horse bus" in a raging blizzard, Lela and Lula were dreading the final mile they would have to walk to get home. They would have to wade through the deep snow that was sure to be on that ungraded stretch of dirt road. Somehow, they convinced themselves that if they got off the bus on the higher, graded gravel road two miles from home, someone would come to meet them with a horse and bobsled so they wouldn't have to walk in the blizzard. They got off the bus and started down the road toward home. They strained to see through the blowing snow, looking for any sign of approaching horses. But, of course, none came. Now, instead of one mile to walk in the blizzard, they had to walk two. To make matters worse, they were heading north, into the wind. The snow and cold stung their faces. The girls turned around and backed into the wind, trying to stay on the road without facing the wind. Lela caught her heel on something and fell backward into the snow. She was completely exhausted from struggling to walk in the snow and from battling the bitter cold. "Just let me lie here and rest a while," she told Lula. "Just a little while." That frightened Lula. She knew that they could freeze to death if they stopped moving. She took hold of Lela's arm and pulled, screaming at her to get up. Lela finally struggled to her feet and the two of them trudged on together, holding their freezing hands over their faces. Somehow they found their neighbor's driveway and made their way to the house. At last, they were safe and could get warm. When they finally got warmed up, they started worrying that someone might be out in the storm looking for them. They didn't want that to happen, so they decided to continue on home. Their neighbors tried to convince them to stay with them, but the girls were too worried. They had to go. Steeling themselves for one last push, they bundled up and went back into the storm. They couldn't see their farm and couldn't see the road, but they knew which direction to head. Going by feel and instinct, they made their way the final quarter mile. The wind let up a little when they reached their farmyard where the grove of trees broke the wind. They hurried to the house and safety. To their astonishment, no one had even discussed going out to look for them! The twins had always gotten home okay before and the storm didn't look that bad from inside the house. They had been completely on their own!

There was not enough money for clothes for everyone, so they had to make do with what they had. They even made use of the cotton cloth from fifty-pound "flour sacks" and "feed sacks". Some of the sacks had flowery print on them just for that purpose. Cut open at the seams, washed and pressed, the sacks yielded somewhat less than a yard of coarse cotton material. Using simple patterns, the sack material was cut and sewn by hand into undergarments. Although not very soft, they were durable. Outer garments were often made from old clothes. Worn-out men's trousers were cut apart and the less worn material from the backs of the legs was used to make skirts. One time, the twins were able to save a little money and bought identical dresses for one dollar each. They were on "cloud nine".

As long as the girls went to the country school, they were comfortable with what they wore. But going to high school in town was a different story. They soon became very self-conscious about their clothes. Young Glen Zeigler made fun of their striped thigh-length stockings and teased the twins about wearing "convict stockings". The teasing embarrassed them and made them even more conscious of the lumps their long underwear made under their long stockings. Sometimes, after they got to school, they would pull their stockings down, roll their long underwear up under their skirts, and then pull the stockings up again. Although it was terribly uncomfortable, they would keep the underwear tucked up under their skirts during the day, then would pull it down and put it back under their stockings on the way home from school. Their mother would have been furious had she known. Although Caroline knew about her sisters' little game, and from time to time would threaten to "tell", she never did -- and their mom never found out.

THE BARN DANCE

Everyone in the Jackson family was excited and filled with anticipation. They had been planning and working hard to get everything ready for the big night. The haymow of the barn was empty and the floor was clean, the food and drinks were ready, the musicians were on their way and the word had been spread. There was going to be a "BARN DANCE" at the Widow Jackson farm.

The Jackson girls had heard about the new "tall, dark and handsome" hired man who was working for their neighbor across the road, but none of them had seen him. The girls wondered if what they had heard about him was true. Was he really "six feet two"? And was he really as strong as they had heard? Also, they wondered if he would come to the dance. There wasn't much in the form of recreation available in 1932 and farm folks from all around would be there to get in on the fun. Everyone was invited. Surely he would come, too.

The barn was alive with people and the musicians were playing when the Smiths' hired man arrived. His name was Bill -- Bill Sloter. As they had heard, he was indeed tall and slim, had dark hair and was ruggedly handsome. He had a relaxed manner, an easy laugh and seemed very self-confident. However, as the evening progressed, they could see that he wasn't much of a dancer. But that didn't keep him from trying. Undeterred by any lack of ability, he danced with many of the young ladies that night, including Lela. She immediately liked his sense of humor, but thought he was a little crude. Other than that, she really didn't give him much thought.

At seventeen, Lela was an attractive young lady. She had bright red hair that fell to her shoulders, with a "spit curl" caressing her forehead. She had a pretty face and a shy, innocent smile that made her especially appealing.

The next day as Bill went about his work, he thought about the dance and the young ladies that he had met there. He thought about the girls with whom he had danced, especially Lela. Her innocent beauty and the way she laughed with him had left a real impression. Since she lived just across the road, maybe he could see her again without "making a big deal of it". That way he could get to know her better without letting her know that she was on his mind. He didn't want anybody "getting ideas" until he was more sure himself.

Every now and then, in the evening after his chores were done or on a Sunday afternoon, Bill would stroll across the road to visit with the Jacksons. He got to know the whole family and enjoyed being with them. And, as he had hoped, he got to know Lela better, as well. He really liked her. She, too, came to secretly look forward to his visits.

On one occasion, Lela was still working cleaning the barn when Bill arrived. He grabbed a pitchfork and began helping her load the spreader. Every now and then, as they talked and pitched manure into the manure spreader, the horses would pull the spreader ahead a little. Whenever that would happen, Lela would shout "whoa" to get them to stop and stand still.

The next night after chores, Bill told his boss, Billy Smith, "I'm going to see my girl. She's pitching shit and hollerin' 'whoa'!"

BILL AND THE BULL

Late one afternoon, Bill was in the barnyard, herding the cows into the barn to be milked, when he heard a dull, galloping sound. Looking around, he saw him coming. The huge herd bull, weighing almost two thousand pounds, was coming toward him at a full gallop. Feeling sudden, overwhelming fear, his muscles tensed and a cold chill ran down his spine. He felt the hair on the back of his neck stand up. Quickly looking around, he located the nearest fence, and ran toward it as fast as he could. Grabbing the top of a post with both hands, he vaulted over the fence and landed on the ground on the other side just as the bull caught up with him and slammed his big head into the fence. His heart racing and completely out of breath, Bill sat for a few minutes on the ground where he had fallen. After catching his breath, he walked over to the barn, sat down and leaned back against the wall to let his nerves settle. He watched as the bull stood pawing the ground and snorting on the other side of the fence.

At that time, almost every farm with cows had a bull or arrangements were made to have a bull brought in, usually from one of the neighbors. Billy Smith chose to have his own bull. By his very nature, a bull is not to be trusted. Many farmers have been killed by a bull they had raised from a calf, and which had not previously shown any signs of aggressive behavior. Suddenly, without warning, they would pin their owner against a fence or a building, or knock him to the ground and gore him to death. Everyone in the area knew Billy Smith's bull was a "mean" bull. Bill had been in the same yard with him many times before and had kept an eye on him. This time he looked away a little too long and was nearly killed because of it.

Bill was twenty years old when he went to work for Billy Smith and was intimidated by no man. It disturbed him greatly that he had run from an animal. The more he thought about it, the more he hated that bull and the fact that he had gotten the best of him. The bull had the upper hand -- Bill was afraid of him! It became a "power struggle" between a man and a beast. Bill vowed, "Someday, I'll teach you who's boss, you big, ugly, son-of-a-bitch!" The beast was coming out in the man.

Sometime later, when the Smiths were gone, Bill was doing chores and the bull was penned up in a small box stall in the barn. Seeing his chance, Bill thought, "Okay, now it's your turn." He went out to the grove and cut a club about the size of a baseball bat, only a little longer. He went with club in hand into the barn and to the bull's stall. The bull snorted around as Bill approached. Bill climbed up on the slatted wall of the stall and, with all the force he could muster, swung the club down on the bull's shoulders. The bull bellowed and Bill hit him again, and again -- and again -- making sure that he hit him where no marks would show later. He hit him across the rump, on the ribs and on the neck. The bull bellowed in pain with every blow as he got a beating he would never forget.

From then on, Bill carried that club with him whenever he walked into the barnyard or to the pasture to get the cows at milking time. The bull kept his distance. More than once the Smiths wondered aloud why the bull never seemed to bother Bill.

Sometime later, the men were putting up hay. Billy and Bill were going through the pasture, riding on top of a hayrack load of hay, when the bull saw Bill without his club and came after him. He circled the rack a few times snorting and pawing the ground. Finally, the enraged bull hooked his horns under the side of the hayrack and threw it into the air. The men grabbed onto the end boards of the rack and held on for dear life. When the rack came down, it landed halfway off the running gear, teetering on the wheels on one side. Somehow, the men managed to stay on the load and out of reach of the bull. But they couldn't go anywhere with one side of the hayrack down on two of the wheels. The bull went around and around the hayrack trying to get at Bill. Finally, Bill moved over near the edge of the hay on the side that was resting on the wheels. The bull ran around to where Bill was standing, hooked his horns under the rack and threw it back on the running gear. It was still a little cockeyed but up off the wheels and good enough to go. Bill grabbed the horses' reins, slapped them down across the horses' backs and hollered "giddy up". The horses took off for home, pulling their light load at a full gallop. The bull followed them for a while, but couldn't keep up as they raced toward the barn. As they bounced across the field, they hoped that the rack wouldn't bounce off the running gear. When he saw that he couldn't catch them, the bull stopped and watched them go. After they got back to the farmyard, Billy said to Bill, "I wonder what got into the bull to make him act like that?" Bill didn't tell him and he never found out. From then on, whenever Bill was in the barnyard or pasture with the bull, whether walking or riding, the club was with him.

A FULL HOUSE

After the crops were planted, Billy Smith decided that he would try to get by without hired help. Bill found himself without a job -- again! The Smiths, like so many farmers at the time, didn't have much money and could no longer afford to pay a man to do work that they could do themselves. Bill offered to do chores and miscellaneous work around the farm for room and board, but even that was out of the question. Bill didn't know where to go to find work. Jobs were scarce.

Bill had become well acquainted with the Jacksons by this time and told them his problem. Minnie suggested that he come to live with them until he could find work. She said that he could do chores and other work around the farm for room and board. Under the circumstances, it was a very generous offer and Bill accepted.

By then, James Jackson had been married to his wife, Clara, for about three years and had two children, Albert and Leonard. James and his family were part of the household living on the farm in the big house. James was still in charge of the overall farming operation.

Minnie's sister had problems that made it impossible for her to care for her son, Robert Ness, so Minnie "took him in", as well. He was about eleven years old when he came to live with the Jacksons.

The hired man, Bill Meyer, who helped the Jacksons move and who worked for them from time to time, also spent some time living with them, working for room and board. Mary, the oldest of the Jackson girls, was seventeen when she and Bill Meyer were married in 1930. They lived on a small farm just down the road from the home place.

Later, when Bill Sloter learned that his younger brother, Ed, was having trouble finding a job, he went to get Ed and brought him back to live with the Jacksons, too, adding yet another member to the "family". At another time, his brother, Ben, also lived with them for a while.

Minnie's children were growing up and some were leaving home, but other people kept moving in. When Lula married Herman Leerar in 1934, the young couple also lived there until they could find a place of their own. So, with all the comings and goings, the "family" seemed to be getting bigger, not smaller.

38

Times were hard and the Jacksons didn't have much but, if someone was in need, Minnie always managed to make room for them. When Bill Sloter took up residence with the Jacksons, there were thirteen people living in the old farmhouse, sleeping where they could find room and eating what was produced on the farm, supplemented with wild game. Even though money was extremely scarce, they lived reasonably well.

THE TWINS

In the spring of 1932, Lela and Lula graduated from Corwith High School with high marks. But a diploma and high marks didn't mean much considering what lay ahead for them on the farm. They were now old enough to be involved in all aspects of field work and that is exactly what was expected. Lela and Lula didn't have the skill or strength to throw the heavy harnesses over the horses' backs, so they had their brother, James, do that for them. Once the harnesses were in place, however, they would do all of the necessary fastening, "hitch up" to whatever implement was to be used that day and head out for a full day in the fields.

The first field work to be done was spring plowing -- that is, finish plowing whatever ground that hadn't been plowed the prior fall. They would ride the sulky plow across the field with one wheel and one horse in the furrow. That was fairly easy because the horses almost guided themselves. Easy, that is, until they would reach the end of the field. At that point, the plow would have to be raised out of the ground with a lever. That would take both hands and all of their strength. Then, after the horses were turned around and in position to go back through the field the other direction, the lever would have to be pulled down, the release squeezed and the plow lowered to the ground, again taking all their strength. It was a man's work, for sure.

Next came disking the plowed ground, then dragging with a four-section drag pulled by four horses, which they would walk behind all day. When the dragging was done, the field was ready to plant. James did the planting because it took special skill to keep the rows straight and to "check" the corn so that it could be cross-cultivated. When the corn was up, it could be rowed (look across the field and see rows) north-south and east-west.

After the corn was up, it needed to be cultivated, usually four times, twice east-west and twice north-south, before cultivating for the last time or "laying it by". That meant being on the cultivator from morning 'til night nearly every day until the corn was too big and would get broken down by the cultivator. The Jacksons had a single-row cultivator that was pulled by a team of horses. The cultivator shovels were on supports that could be swung from side to side, but not back and forth. There were metal stirrups on the supports. The operator would sit on a steel seat with a foot resting in each of the stirrups, guiding the shovels around the corn plants while driving the horses as they pulled the cultivator through the field. It was a very tiring job, especially for a young woman. Field work also included "making hay" and getting it into the haymow, cutting, shocking and thrashing oats, and picking corn by hand in the fall.

In the fall of 1933, after the harvesting was done, Billy Smith's wife, Hannah, went into the hospital for surgery. The Smiths needed someone to help on the farm during the time Hannah was in the hospital and while she was recovering at home. They went to the Jacksons to see if any of them could help out. After the family discussed the matter, it was agreed that Lela would go there to work. She was paid room and board and two dollars per week -- very low wages, even then. That was Lela's first job "working out".

Even considering the low wages, having a job away from home sounded good to Lela, but she soon learned that it was no vacation. She cooked the meals, washed the dishes, cleaned the house, helped their daughter, Francis, fix her hair for school, and did the family's washing and ironing. In addition to all that, Billy expected her to do outside work such as cleaning the chicken house and barn! Wanting to please her employer, she did what he asked, working very hard to get everything done. She went to bed exhausted at the end of each day.

When Hannah Smith was well enough to begin doing her own work, she told Lela that she would like to "keep her on", but that they just couldn't afford it. Although she wouldn't be earning cash money, Lela was secretly happy to be going home.

As in almost all families, there was sibling rivalry in the Jackson family. The twins were sometimes teased that they each were just "half a person", and that they should get only half as much of anything as the other children in the family. But, of course, they were each expected to do their share of the work, which they did.

Lela and Lula had a very close, and very special, relationship. They shared almost everything. Whenever something was bought for one, each would see to it that the other got it, as well. On one occasion, Lela spent a week's pay for each of them to have a new pair of gloves. If there wasn't enough money to buy whatever they wanted for the both of them, they just wouldn't buy it. Growing up, Lela and Lula learned the value of money, of setting goals and of working hard to achieve those goals. They learned to unselfishly sacrifice themselves for the benefit of others. This caring, self-sacrificing quality that they developed at a young age stayed with them throughout their lives.

The twins, Lula (left) and Lela

COURTSHIP

Bill enjoyed his stay at the Jacksons in 1932. He was there for a few weeks during which time he helped with various tasks around the farm to "pay his way" and in order to feel comfortable accepting their hospitality. He especially enjoyed hunting pheasants and rabbits. Almost every day, he would take the family "22" rifle and go hunting in the surrounding fields and road ditches. Bill was a crack shot, often hitting pheasants on the fly or rabbits on the run with the rifle. Bill always seemed to bring game home to add to the next meal. It was a carefree and enjoyable time for him.

But, before long, Bill got itchy feet. He needed a job. He soon found work with the McEnroe brothers on one of their farms near Algona, Iowa. Permanent jobs working on a farm were almost non-existent at that time and that job was not permanent either. After finishing there, he went from place to place in Iowa, Minnesota and Illinois, working wherever he could find employment.

By this time, Bill's mother had moved back to Eureka, Illinois, where she had grown up and where her family still lived. The Sloter side of the family lived near Eureka and Dixon, Illinois. Bill went to visit them in August, 1932. He wrote his first letter to Lela Jackson from there on August 23, 1932. She said, "I wasn't all that excited about receiving mail from that big character." But she tucked his letter away and kept it, anyway. The letter was eventually lost, but she still had the envelope.

This is Bill's second letter to Lela:

Rudd Iowa
D. S. Kuper, Special Agent   Sept 7, 1932.
New York Life Insurance Co.
Telephone: 3-F-35 Rudd, Iowa

Dear Lela Jackson.
Well how is every little thing by this
time. I am here with an old friend now
an I think I'll be there in a day or so. I
suppose you have been looking for a
letter for a long time. Well I did not
have time to write. Having so much
fun. I may see you fri day or sat..day.
You can answer this letter By writing
to Algona Ia. o/o Mc Enroe Bros. I
suppose you almost thought I had
forgot you by this time. Well kid I can't
think of much to write But Will tell you
more when I see you again. How is
every body out   that way by this time.
The adress above is my friend up here.
have been here a Week. Driving his
car for him.
XXXX Well I guess I'll close hoping to
OOOO see you real soon. as Ever Bill
Sloter

(Lela's comment about this letter: *"That part about having so much fun was 'bullshit'. There wasn't anything to have fun at in those days!"*)

Bill got a job working for Ed Bailey in Alden, Minnesota, in the fall of 1932. His next letter to Lela was sent from there.

Alden, Minnesota
Oct 8 1932

Dear Lela.
Well I supose you think I have forgot
you By this time. Well how is every
little thing By this time. an how is
Every body out that Way Well I supose.
Does anybody need an Corn picker out
thatWay if so let me know. An I Will be
outon see you soon as possible annway.
Or mabe you folks will need a hand in the
spring as I seen long in algona an he
said Jim has a farm rented. So please
Write an let me know How you all are an
if you still love me. Hoping to hear from
you real soon Honey.

Same as Ever Bill Sloter
Alden Minn
o/o Ed Bailey
X X X X X X X
X X X X X
X O O O O O O

By By ans Soon

December 23, 1932 found Bill in Minneapolis. He sent a Christmas card to Lela from there.

Dear Lela J.
Will I am in Minn Right now But am
going to St Cloud. Now How is
everybody Just fine I hope as ever before
Your Best Pal. So I guess I'll colse
Sweethear Dear
O X
Mr Wm Sloter.

Steady jobs were impossible to find, but I suspect that Bill enjoyed a break from work every now and then. He liked to do "piece work" because he could earn more money that way and this allowed him freedom to visit around "between jobs".

45

It took unusual skill and stamina to pick one hundred bushels of corn in a day. To most men, it was just a dream. In the following letter, Bill mentions picking one hundred bushels easily.

Eureka Ill.
Jan 12, 1933

Darling Lela. Well how are
you by this time. I am fine
at present I am picking corn
an Will be here about a Week.
I supose you think I am never
going to Write any more
But have been very Busy.
So you can answer right
away an I will get it.
How is every body up there
by this time. May see you
in abought two Weeks.
I am up at my Grandmothers
place right now. I supose you
are having good time With
out me up there. Well have
your fun I am having mine.
Well dear I don't know Much
to write But Will scrible a
little more. I sent you a card
from minn did you get it. Say
you send me a good picture of
your self as Grand ma Wants
to see What you look like. I
am going to send you a
picture of my self an my sister
Katherine an one of Esther.
The Weather is cold up here
but We have no snow. at
present but looks like rain.
The corn is making about 85
bu. to an acre up here.
Sure can pick a 100 Bu easy.
But only getting 2c a bu. an it
Wont last Very much longer.

Say honey do you still love
Me Write an let me know.
Ha Ha. Did Joe go home for
Xmas. I didnot. But I saw all
the folks at church. Good
Boy Ha.Ha. Well sweet heart I
guaess I Will close I am going
to bed now. I am Sleeping
With My cousin Elsie. Ha.Ha.
Well honey yours till oceans
wear Rubber pants to keep
there Bottoms dry.
Mr Wm Sloter. Eureaka Ill.
o/o Mrs Louis Sloter
B. S. answer soon.
B.live. u.   L.ove L.ove.
S.ister H.anna I,s. T.uly.
HELLo. Honey good By.
X X X X X X X X X X X
X X X X X X X X X X X
O O O O O O O O O X X.

(The above letter displays some of Bill's sense of humor. Notice the first letter of each of the eight words before sign-off. They spell "BuLL SHIT".)

Jan 30, 1933
Dixon Ill
Darling Lela. Just a few
words to say Hello. I am
not feeling very good the
last couple days. May be
back real soon. Well honey
the weather sure is cold up
here. I have seen all I am
going to see this time. I
guess, I will not be here
very long so don't answer.
Lots + lots of Love Bill

Bill worked from time to time with his cousin Jack Johnson and Jack's father hauling coal in Dixon, Illinois. It was hard work, but he liked his uncle and cousin and enjoyed being with them.

Dixon Ill.
Mar 30, 1933.

Darling Lela.
Well I ricived your letter an was glad
to hear from you. I guiss Ill be here
quite a while yet. as I do not know when
I can make any more money than I can
up here. So James has moved. Well I
went to work up here about two months
ago.   No I have not been to any dances
up here. But have been having a lot of
fun anyway. Say kid how come you
didn,t send me a picture of yourself. As
I would love to have one of them. Well
how are all the rest of the folks By this
time. Well honey I am working Every
day now But don,t know how long it
Will last as the fellow I am Working
With Wants me to By a share in The
company. But I can,t hardly do that as I
have not the money to invest But Will be
seeing you one of these days When ever
my Job comes to an end. Well honey I
don,t know much to write But will try an
do Better next time. My cousin Jack
Wants to say Hello. Well tell Every
body Hello for me. The Weather Is
rainie up here. But Not Very cold. Well
Kid I sure Would like to be With you
tonight But I guess that is imposible. so
I Wont say any More about It.
Well honey don,t forget to send me a
picture of your self.
  Yours till oceans Ware Rubber pants to
keep there Bottoms dry.
X X X X X X X X X X
Your Pal
Mr Wm Sloter
        Dixon Ill
            o/o David Emmert
            R 4 Box 1

48

Bill went to visit Lela with his brother, Ben, and the Hendricks brothers, George and Ben. Bill normally traveled by "hopping a freight" train, "hitching a ride" on the road and by walking. This time the Hendricks brothers drove their car from Minnesota to meet Lela.

When they got to the Jacksons, Lela was out bringing the cows in from the pasture. Bill sent his brother, Ben, who looked a lot like Bill, out to meet her, pretending to be Bill. Lela wasn't fooled in the least, but they got a good laugh out of it.

o/o Ray. Hanon
Glenville Minn
Oct 12, 1933

Darling Lela:
Recived your letter a day or so ago
an was glad to hear from you. The
Weather is mild up here at present.
an I hope is Remains so for a few
days. I am going to start husking
corn Monday. Tell your ma I Will
Husk for her after I get done here.
An I can Wait for my pay if she is
short of money. An please Write an
let me know What she says about.
it. Well honey Wish I was there
With you But I promised this guy I
Would pick his corn an I don't like
to go bank on my Word. So I guess
I Will stay here till I get throu
picking his corn an then I Will be
able to see you more often. No you
weren,t very friendly but I know it
is my fault. so I just loved you same
as I ever did. Well honey I know I
stayed away a long time. But I can
explain it all. An for another thing I
had nothing to do With any other
girls as long as I Was gone. An say
I Wish you would not step out with
any more guys till I get back
because I really do care for you

more then I ever did any one else
Say honey my Bro tought you Wer
swell. But George an Ben Hendricks
didn,t say any thing as they Were
sore Because it Was so far over
there. Say Dear I have a chance to By
a good car for a $100.00 But I am
$20 short. an this guy Wants cash. so
I guess I Won,t Buy it. Say honey
Don,t ever let any Body Make you
think I am trying to make a fool of you
as I am not. that kind of a guy. an if I
Was do you supose I Would Drive a
Hundred miles to see you. an as you
Was saying about getting married. I
will most likely see you getting
married to Somebody I know Perty
Well. So I guess I,ll close for this time
Your loving pal Bill an Feautue
Husband.
X X X X X X X X X X X X X X X X X X
say honey send me one of them frame
pictures. an I will Bring it Back When
come up.
   Don,t forget.

              Glenville, Minn
               Nov. 2, 1933

Dear Lela.
Well how are you By this time I got
your letter an was glad to hear from you
The Weather has Benn Warm up here I
think I,ll see you by the 13th of the Mo.
If the Weather stays fit tio pick corn.
Well Honey I Went to Albert lea sunday
an helped my uncle say Wood. Guess
I'll pick corn this coming sunday. So I'll
get done by the 12th. As I am getting
lonesome for you mabe you are getting
lonesome for me to. Ha Ha. So I hope to

see you then. Well honey my hands are
sore from picking corn So I Wont Write
Very much tonite. Tell every body hello
for me. an I will come up as soom as I
can get away from here.
Answer Real soon.
    X X X X X X X excuse Writing
      Lots + Lots of love.
      Mr Wm Sloter
      o/o Ray hanon.

                  Glenville Minn
                  Nov 10 1933

      Darling Lela..
       I Recived your
      letter an Was glad to
      here from you. Well
      I am getting done pick-
      corn an my kid Bro.
      Is here With me.
      an We can get more
      picking But if your
      ma Wants us to
      pick for her We Will
      be there monday morn.
      So Write at once an
      let me know What
      she says. Well
      honey I guess I,ll
      come up there an pick
      for you folks. Well
      I guess Ill close for
      to night an Will
      see you next Week.
      When I can tell you
      more.
         your Pal Bill
       Lots an lots of
       love.
       ans. Soon

MARRIAGE AND FAMILY

Bill's persistent expressions of love and affection for Lela eventually paid off. Gradually, she came to welcome -- even look forward to -- his letters. She pondered the proposal of marriage made in his letter to her dated October 12, 1933, when she was working for Billy Smith. By mid-summer, 1934, she had decided to accept his proposal. Bill, Lela, Minnie and Bill's brother, Earl, drove to Sioux Falls, South Dakota, where Bill Sloter and Lela Jackson were married by a justice of the peace on July 18, 1934. Minnie and Earl "stood up" for them.

By that time, James Jackson and his family had moved to their own place, so Bill took over managing the 320-acre Widow Jackson farm. Bill and Lela both worked outside at whatever needed doing to farm the land and to manage the farm operation. The two of them even picked all of the corn by hand.

Picking corn efficiently required a wagon with sideboards about two feet high on one side, a good team of horses, husking gloves and a husking hook that was strapped on over the glove.

The team of horses, once started, would pull the wagon straight down the corn row, needing only an occasional "giddy up" or "whoa", from whomever was picking, to move the wagon along as they picked their way across the field. To pick an ear of corn, a person would reach down, gripping the ear with one hand and twisting downward, breaking it loose from the stalk. Holding the ear in one hand, the husking hook on the other hand was used to remove the husk from the ear before throwing it against the bangboard and into the wagon. With practice, this all became one fluid motion. A skilled corn picker, picking two rows at a time, could move quickly enough to keep one or two ears "in the air" at all times, enabling him to pick one hundred or more bushels a day. Bill was able to do that.

For their work, Lela and Bill were paid room and board plus $17.00 per month. Even though that wasn't much pay, they felt a sense of security there on the farm.

Although Lela was pregnant at the time, she worked right alongside Bill doing all types of field work and harvesting crops. Doctors say that a pregnant woman should get exercise to have an easy delivery and a healthy baby. Lela was certainly getting enough exercise!

In December, 1934, after the harvesting was done and work slowed down on the farm, Bill took time off to go visit his mother. Still without transportation of their own, Bill hitchhiked to Eureka, Illinois. Lela stayed home because it would have been very difficult for her to travel the way Bill did, plus she was needed on the farm. She never even considered going.

Eureka Ill.
Dec 12, 1934

Dear Wife
Well honey I got
Here about five o'clock
Tues, Had good luck in
Getting up here I haven't
Seen Ma yet. But
Am going up to see
Here today I guess.
They haven't any
Snow. Up here at
All. seems like summer.
Tell Ed I seen clarnce
an he is a lot Better
looking than he is.
Well honey I,ll be back
soon as I can or if
you don,t miss me
I may stay longer
Well tell everyone
Hello for me.
I supose its as
cold as ever up there. Well Honey
I don,t know much
to Write so I guess I,ll close.
Tell Gladys I sure fell Bad that
I couldn,t kiss
her good by. Ha.Ha.

Well honey good
by an good luck.
With lots of
love for all.

Your Husband Bill.

Bill sent a Christmas card to Lela from Dixon, Illinois, on December 16, 1934.

Dear Wife an family.
Well how are you
all by this time I am
fine an hope you are
the same. Well hony
I supose you miss
me an aful lot Dont
you Well I guess I,ll
be back monday
or tues. Well I saw
ma an lots of the
others an sure am
having fun. Well
tell every body hello
for me. Well I guess
Ill close for this
time Bill.

One morning, soon after Bill got home from Illinois, Lela was having stomach pains and told him that she couldn't work that day, and that maybe it was "time". Dr. Judd was called out to the farm from his office in Kanawha to deliver Bill and Lela's first child, a healthy baby boy. They named him James William after Lela's brother James and the baby's father, Bill. I entered the world the morning of January 24, 1935, in an upstairs bedroom of the old farmhouse.

Mom was soon back on her feet working right alongside Dad, doing the same things around the farm that she did before I was born. Over the ensuing months, she helped to prepare the fields, plant and cultivate, and then helped to harvest the crops in the fall.

The fall harvest was over and the 1935 fall plowing almost done. Mom was well into her second pregnancy and it was progressing normally. That is, until one day when she went to the barn alone to harness the team. She went into the horse stall between the two large horses she had been using every day in the field. Reaching up to put the halter on the mare so she could lead it out of the stall, she happened to touch the mare's shoulder where it had been rubbed raw by the harness collar. The mare swung her head around and hit Mom, knocking her off balance, and then reared over toward the other horse, squeezing Mom between them. When the horses moved apart, Mom fell to the ground beneath them. By that time, both horses were excited and began kicking and stomping around. Mom tried to get to her hands and knees to crawl out, but they kept kicking her and knocking her down, again and again. There just happened to be a narrow doorway, in the side of the stall, leading into an alleyway. Mom managed to reach out and grab hold of the doorframe and pull herself from under the horses and through the doorway to safety, away from the flailing hooves. In pain, she lay there for a while on the barn floor, gathering strength, before struggling to her feet and slowly making her way to the house.

Mom didn't go to a doctor, but the family examined her as best they could and determined that, although she had multiple bruises and several broken ribs, there seemed to be no other injury. Luckily, the horses had only kicked her in the body and not her head, and had not stomped on her. Mom's ribs hurt so much that she could hardly breathe. With every movement, it felt as though someone was stabbing her with a knife. She couldn't straighten up without severe pain, so she walked stooped over for several weeks until she began to heal. She worried about the baby, though, and watched fearfully for any signs of trouble. There were none and, as time passed, and as her ribs and bruises began to heal, her fears subsided.

By 1935, the economy was beginning to improve. Grandma Jackson had done quite well farming on her own over the previous eight years and decided to buy a farm. She found one that looked good to her, and at a low price, nearly two hundred miles away in west central Minnesota, near Morris, and made a down payment. She knew that the farm she was buying wasn't as good as the one she was renting, but it wouldn't have to be at the price she was paying.

Grandma gave up the farm near Corwith and made preparations to move everything she had to her new farm. The moving process was begun by moving farm machinery in mid-February so the move would be completed by March 1, 1936. By the third week of February, most of the equipment had been moved, but moving the livestock and household furnishings would have to wait until the first of March. Moving to another farm was hectic, especially when it was so far away. Each family had to be out of the house they were in and the livestock out of the farm buildings to make room for the family and livestock moving in on the same day. And the weather didn't always cooperate.

The winter of 1935/1936 went on record as one of the century's worst winters in the Midwest. While in the midst of moving, Mom, Dad and Grandma Jackson stayed with Mom's sister, Caroline, and her family. They lived just down the road from the home place.

It was near the end of February, during one of the year's worst blizzards, that Mom again told Dad she thought it was "time". Dr. Wally, in Corwith, was called and they prayed that he could get to the farm in time. Dr. Wally left his office immediately after being called, hitched the horses to his buggy and headed out of town. The minute he reached the edge of Corwith the doctor realized he had a problem. There was blowing snow and huge drifts everywhere. It was a full-blown blizzard and impossible to go by road. So he left the road and crossed fields, cutting fences as he went, to make his way to the farm five miles away. The wind would let up every now and then so the doctor could see which way to go. He was thoroughly familiar with the area around Corwith so, if he could see at all, he wouldn't get lost.

The family watched and waited for the doctor while Mom's labor pains grew stronger and more frequent. Mom was lying in bed on her side, trying to wait, when finally Dad said, "You just as well roll over and have it, 'cuz the doctor isn't going to get here." Finally, Mom had no choice. Dad and Grandma Jackson delivered a healthy baby boy two hours before the doctor arrived. My brother, Julian, was born the morning of February 26, 1936. Julian was a big baby -- eight pounds and twelve ounces, Mom said -- and Mom tore when he was born. When Dr. Wally asked her if she wanted a painkiller before he stitched her up, Mom said, "No, if I stood this much, I guess I can stand a little more." Dr. Wally charged $17.00 for his services that day.

Mom and the new baby stayed in Iowa with Aunt Caroline and Uncle Joe for a few weeks while everyone else went to Minnesota. When Mom's stitches healed and she felt strong enough to travel, Dad went to Iowa and brought her and Julian home to the new farm in Minnesota. Mom continued to work outside right alongside Dad on the farm in Minnesota. The crops there were poor compared to the crops in Iowa, but they managed to get by.

Two years after Julian was born, Mom became pregnant with her third child. In July, 1938, she began to feel uneasy. She knew that her delivery time was getting close, but somehow she wasn't comfortable. She became anxious about the baby. She didn't feel the same as she had with the other two pregnancies and it bothered her. She became increasingly uncomfortable and had intermittent pains for three days. When the pains became more frequent and severe, Dad called a doctor in Morris, Minnesota, to come to the farm. He said he would be there -- but he didn't come! They waited. Mom's pains kept getting worse and still they waited, but he still didn't come. Dad called again and finally the doctor came to the farm. But he was there only a short time when he said he needed to go back to town, and left. He didn't come back! Agitated by this time, Dad jumped in Grandma's old car and drove to Morris to the doctor's office and brought the doctor back to the farm with him. That time, he stayed (he would have had to get past Dad to leave) and delivered a normal, healthy baby boy. Our brother, Don, was born July 10, 1938.

One of my earliest memories is of Christmas, 1938, when I was almost four. Someone brought a big cardboard box into the kitchen and set it on the floor. It was full of toys for "us kids" and there was a set of dishes for Mom. I couldn't believe so many toys. We took them out of the box and spread them out on the kitchen floor. I especially liked the large metal top that whistled when it was spun by quickly and repeatedly pushing down on the handle in the center. The gifts were from the doctor who had been so slow to respond to my parents' call. He apparently had some type of personal problem that had prevented him from responding to the call in a professional manner. The gifts were seen as his way of saying, "I'm sorry," to Mom and to our family.

HURLING CLODS

As her horses got older, "Grandma" Jackson was forced to buy more to replace those that could no longer work. As was often the case when buying or trading horses, she couldn't be sure of what she was getting. Had she or Dad known, she would never have owned one good-looking animal, a large "bay" that Dad bought for her at auction. They learned later that as a young colt, he had injured a hip when he and another horse went through a barn door at the same time. They called him "Hippy".

One day, Mom hitched Hippy, along with three other horses, to a four-section drag harrow and went to the field. With reins in hand, she walked behind as the horses pulled the drag across the field. They hadn't gone far when the big bay stopped. Mom hollered "giddy up", but Hippy just stood there. Finally, she picked up a baseball-size clod of dirt and threw it, hitting the balky horse in the rump. He moved and they were on their way again across the field -- but not for long. Soon he stopped again. But this time, he lay down and got tangled up in his harness. "What a mess that was!" Somehow, Mom managed to unhitch him and get his harness untangled, hitch him up again and start across the field. The next time the big bay tried to stop, she was ready for him. Holding the four reins in her left hand, Lela reached down and picked up a baseball-size clod of dirt in her right hand and threw it, again striking him on the rump. He flinched, did a little jump and kept going. So that became the routine. Whenever the big bay would slow down, Lela would throw a clod of dirt at him to prod him on. It worked. He never did get a chance to lie down in his harness again. But that added effort, along with walking behind the drag and driving the horses, made for very long, strenuous days in the field.

By the end of the day, Mom was completely exhausted -- and she still had to unhitch the horses, take the harnesses off and hang them on the hook in the barn, then rub the horses down and feed them.

"God, I hated that horse!"

UNDUE FORCE

After she had given "us kids" a bath, Mom got out our 'Sunday best' clothes and helped Julian and me get dressed. After she dressed baby Don, she stood me on a chair and combed my hair. It was late in the day, when we would normally be getting ready for bed. But instead, we were getting dressed up to go someplace. I asked Mom where we were going. "Something happened to your Dad," she said. "We're going to see him in the hospital." She didn't tell us what had happened. I was only three years old, but I remember it very well. It was a traumatic experience for me.

For some reason, the city policeman in Morris, Minnesota displayed an intense dislike for both Dad and Mom. There may have been something Dad had said or done in the past that caused the policeman to feel as he did, and to feel justified in harassing my parents. That is not known. But for some reason, whenever he saw either Mom or Dad drive Grandma's old car into town, he would follow them and pull them over for any reason he could concoct. Mom was afraid to drive into town for fear of being "picked up". "He would 'pick us up' for no reason at all."

Dad had "gone to town" on Saturday night, in Morris, and had stopped at the local tavern. When Dad came out of the tavern and got into the car, that policeman seemed to appear out of nowhere. Dad rolled the window down and asked the policeman what he wanted. The policeman pulled out a teargas gun, placed the barrel against Dad's right cheek, and said, "Start the car and get out of town." Whether what happened next was an accident or not, is not known. But the teargas gun discharged. The projectile and chemical penetrated Dad's face. In shock and in terrible pain, Dad drove out of town toward home. The policeman must have immediately radioed the highway patrol. A patrolman intercepted Dad on the road not far from the farm. He loaded Dad into his patrol car and took him to the hospital. He also arranged to have someone notify Mom and take our family to the hospital to see Dad.

"His face was all puffed up. It was really a mess."

59

Dad wore a bandage on his face for several days after he came home. The swelling eventually went down and the bandage was removed. The wound should have been healed by the time they took the bandage off, but it wasn't. The chemicals in the teargas must have done permanent damage to the skin and muscle tissue in that area, because the wound never did heal. The small, dark-colored hole about the size of a pencil eraser "wept" constantly.

Mom and Dad tried to ignore the wound that wouldn't heal, and they did for several years. Eventually, the weeping seemed to increase and a hard mass began developing under the skin. My parents worried that it would develop into cancer. Dad went to the doctor and was told that surgery should be done to 'clean it out'. He went into the hospital as an outpatient, expecting it to be a quick operation. The surgery ended up taking several hours and required a much larger incision than was originally planned. A tumor with "fingers" had developed and had spread over a large portion of his right cheek and into his upper lip. The surgeon did a good job and the incision healed properly afterward.

The tumor was gone, but Dad carried a two-inch crescent-shaped scar on his right cheek for the rest of his life. Also, the muscles in his right cheek were permanently damaged. When he smiled, it only showed in his eyes and on the left side of his face. He had a "crooked smile". The incident had truly disfigured him.

The policeman had definitely used undue force. My parents could have brought suit against the police, but the thought never even occurred to them. Charges were never filed against the policeman for what he did to my Dad.

CHANGES

The farm Grandma bought in Minnesota wasn't rich and fertile like the farm she had rented in Iowa. There was no comparison. Farming the hard rocky soil of that farm was much more difficult and the crops weren't nearly as good. In fact, they never did have a good corn crop 'up there'. The ears were mostly just "nubbins" that didn't fill out. Each year seemed to be more of a struggle than the year before. It was virtually impossible for Grandma to make any progress on the farm debt. Grandma's youngest daughter, Alma, got married to Darrell (Red) Stockwell at age sixteen and left the farm. Gladys was now the only daughter yet unmarried and she was away at college, studying to be a teacher. Minnie's family was all grown and on their own. Grandma began to see farming that farm and trying to pay for it as "fighting a losing battle". What was the purpose now that she didn't have children to support? Besides, with the "kids" gone, the workload was just too much for her and for Mom and Dad. Grandma was tired. She anguished over her situation and finally decided to just stop trying. She quit farming, sold everything on a farm auction and let the farm "go back" in the spring of 1939.

That decision meant major changes for Grandma and for my family. Grandma's life became much simpler and quite nomadic. First, she went to Iowa where all her children were living and moved in with Alma and "Red" to do what she could to help them get started with married life. From there, she went to live with Caroline and Joe for awhile, then Lula and Herman, and later with others of her children whenever they needed a helping hand. A willing worker and pleasant to have around, she was always welcome wherever she went. Eventually, "Gram" went to work as a housekeeper for Harold Nielson, a bachelor who farmed near the old home place in Iowa.

After Grandma gave up the farm, Dad was without a job for the first time in several years. Mom had kept a cow and calf from her 4-H Club project when she was in high school. They were both sold on the farm sale, so Mom and Dad had a little money to go on. Dad found a steady "job on the farm" working for Mark McGuire near Algona, Iowa. However, it turned out to be something other than what he had expected. Dad was no longer managing a farm operation and had no control over what he did or when he did it. He soon became dissatisfied with the heavy workload of field work and milking. It required him to work from early morning until late into the evening every day to get it all done.

One day, while Dad was at work, Mom took us kids with her to pick wild grapes that grew along the fence beside a road ditch. She pressed the grapes and fermented the juice into homemade wine. After it had fermented for a few weeks, Mom tasted it and thought it was delicious. She had Dad taste it when he came home that night. He liked it, too. A few days later, Mom came to the house and found Dad standing outside, leaning on the yard fence, staring off into space. He was holding a near-empty tumbler of the "green" wine in his hand. Dad looked at Mom with eyes glassy from drink and said, "I think I'll quit." Mom protested and Dad went back to work that afternoon building fence, which was probably the one farm job he hated most.

"That wine must have packed quite a wallop, because that fence was crookeder than hell," Mom would say later.

Dad had time to think while he worked and decided to quit, whether Mom thought he should or not. Dad waited until the chores were finished that night before saying anything to his boss.

"You can't do that," the boss said. "You have a family." "Like hell I can't," Dad answered. He walked back to the tenant house and began making preparations to move -- with no place to go. Somehow, Dad located an old vacant tenant house on a farm near the little town of Seneca, Iowa, and moved us in. It was a tiny, one-room house, but it provided shelter for the five of us and Mom was glad to have it. Dad did odd jobs around the farm place to pay for living there.

"Food was not a problem."

Mom was always canning and preserving food that was in abundance at the time, whether it be pork from the portion of a hog received as pay, beef, chicken or produce from the garden. She canned sweet corn, beans, peas, carrots, applesauce, tomatoes and pickles, and also made her own ketchup. Dad was a good hunter and game was abundant. He was always able to bring home a pheasant, a rabbit, or an occasional squirrel. My parents bought a year's supply of potatoes at a time. They only had to buy flour and a few other basics that couldn't be produced on the farm to have good meals. Dad always did the shopping in those early years. Sometimes he had produce to trade and was confident that he could bargain better than Mom. We had plenty to eat.

One afternoon our family was sitting around the kitchen table -- except baby Donnie, who was playing on the floor. He had crawled around behind the cook stove. Mom turned to see what he was doing and started screaming. She jumped up, grabbed something away from him and picked him up. Apparently, he had found the eight-ounce can of kerosene which was used to start fires in the stove, and which had been placed behind the stove leg. He had drunk from it before anyone realized what he was doing! Mom immediately became panicky and wasn't sure what to do. Looking around, she saw a container of milk setting on the table. She grabbed it and practically poured the milk down Don's throat, shouting, with panic in her voice, "Drink"! Don drank. She kept hollering, almost screaming, "Drink some more!" again and again. He gulped the milk. Soon, he began to vomit. With Don in Mom's arms, my parents ran outside, jumped in the car and rushed him to the doctor. The doctor checked Don over and told them that what Mom had done had saved his life, but that he wasn't safe yet. He could develop pneumonia. They were told to watch him closely for the next few days. Don was sick with a high temperature for nearly a week, then gradually began to improve. Thankfully, a tragedy had been averted.

Mom and Dad liked the young farm family, the Jensens, who lived in the main house on the farm. They enjoyed spending evenings with them, visiting and playing cards. We lived there through the winter of 1939. When the spring of 1940 came, the house was needed for their summer hired man. Dad had to find a job and a place for us to go. He went to work for a farmer northwest of Britt, Iowa, for a dollar a day on an "as needed" basis. We moved again. That move proved to be the most temporary yet. The farmer's wife treated our family like "dirt under her feet". She even went so far as to report to the Hancock County Relief Office that we had moved there from Kossuth County. Because of the move, if my parents were to ask for help from Hancock County, we wouldn't get any. Mom and Dad learned what had happened from the county official when he came to the farm to "serve papers" on us. It really didn't make any difference to Mom and Dad, though. They weren't about to ask the county for help. Their pride wouldn't let them. "It was the principle of the thing." But what the farmer's wife had done really upset them. The "crowning blow" for Dad came when the farmer handed him the agreed-upon one-dollar pay for the day's work and said, "Here's your dollar. You didn't earn it, but here it is." Within weeks of moving there, we were moving again. By that time, Mom had quit unpacking. She left the dishes and silverware in an old copper boiler with a lid on it. Everything else was kept in boxes set around the walls of the room. The frequent moving was made somewhat easier by the fact that we had very little furniture. All we had for household furnishings were a cook stove, a kitchen table and chairs, two beds, and a baby bed.

ILLINOIS

One day, Dad and Uncle James went to Corwith and stopped at the "pool hall". The brothers-in-law had been there drinking beer and talking for a few hours when Dad mentioned that he wished he could see his mother in Illinois. Uncle James said, "I would like to see my sister, Mary, too. Why don't we go see them both. I'll buy half of the gas and help drive." Without telling anyone they were going, the two men got in Dad's Model B Ford and headed for Illinois. Mary and her husband, Bill Meyer, lived southeast of St. Louis, in Percy, Illinois, about five hundred and fifty miles away. Grandma Sloter was in Eureka, Illinois, a little over two hundred miles north of there. The men decided to go to Mary and Bill's first, then to Grandma's. Driving through the night, they arrived in Percy the next morning, out of money, nearly out of gas and a long way from home.

After visiting Bill and Mary on their farm for a couple days, Dad and Uncle James headed north toward Eureka with a full stomach and a nearly empty gas tank. Fortunately, the Model B was in good condition, so the only thing they had to worry about was gas. Dad always carried mechanics hand tools along. With no money, and no way to get any, Dad decided to see if he could trade tools for gas. After several tries, he found a station owner who would allow him a fair price for some of his tools and got the tank filled. A full tank would take them to Eureka and part way home from there. They would worry about getting enough gas to get the rest of the way home when the time came.

Besides wanting to see his mother, Dad had another reason for going to visit her. He wanted Mom to work with him picking up potatoes and onions and to help him pick corn in the fall. They would need a baby sitter. Dad hoped his mother would help out and wanted to ask her "face-to-face".

When their men didn't come home from town, Mom and Aunt Clara got together, each of them thinking that her husband was at the other's place. When they discovered that the men weren't at either place, they began asking around. No one knew anything about where they might be. All the women could do was pray that nothing had happened to their husbands and wait for them to show up.

Dad had a steady job doing chores for Studers, which amounted to milking about twenty cows and pail-feeding eight calves morning and night. Mom had no choice but to do those chores herself while Dad was away. Fortunately, Dad's younger brother, Ed, was staying with us, so he took care of us kids while Mom was out of the house.

After visiting with Grandma for awhile, Dad told her what he had in mind and asked her if she would come home with him. She agreed and packed her suitcase. They loaded into the car and headed for Iowa. About half way home, the car was low on gas again. Grandma wasn't carrying any money, so Dad couldn't borrow from her. Again, he was able to trade tools to fill the tank and they were on their way. When Dad and Uncle James finally arrived home, Mom was relieved but, at the same time, very angry. She couldn't believe what Dad had done without talking it over with her first.

"It was nuts!"

Still, she was very glad to have him home.

THE MODEL "B"

When Grandma sold the farm, our family needed a car. Dad bought a good-looking old Nash that ran well and had plenty of room for our family. The old, square-bodied car was dependable and didn't give any trouble, but they soon learned that it was a real gas-guzzler. "It would pass everything on the road but a gas station!"

"We couldn't afford to go anyplace with it."

Dad "kept his eyes open" for something better and eventually came across a 1933 Model B Ford in a used car lot. The Model B looked like a streamlined Model A and was Ford's first car with a V-8 engine. Even though it was eight years old, the little Ford was in almost new condition. It was love at first sight. Dad made a deal and traded cars. It was a proud day when he drove into the yard with our "new car". Mom and "the kids" gathered around as he showed it off. I was five years old at the time, but I remember him opening the driver's door, reaching in and turning on the ignition and pushing the starter button. It roared to life and "ran like a watch". Standing on the ground beside the car, Dad reached in with his right foot and pressed down on the "foot feed" to "rev up" the engine. Grinning from ear to ear, he said, "Just listen to that. Doesn't she run nice?"

It was potato harvest time about a year later. Mom and Dad decided to earn some money picking up potatoes until Dad could find a steady job. They found a job working in the potato fields for "Kennedy Vegetables and Livestock" west of Clear Lake, Iowa. They drove our "new car" back and forth to the job from where we lived, west of Woden, Iowa.

One morning on the way to work near Clear Lake, Mom said, "This is a really nice car. I think we should keep it for a long time." The sun was just coming up and they were looking directly into it as they drove east on the graveled country roads. Not five minutes later at an intersection just west of Woden, they met a truck, loaded with chickens, going north on its way to market. Dad slammed on the brakes and swerved to miss the truck.

"It was like a nightmare! We were sliding into the path of the truck and the truck kept coming."

They collided with a terrible crash and both vehicles ended up overturned in the ditch. Mom and Dad managed to push the passenger door open and climb out of the smashed ruins of their car. Miraculously, neither was injured. The driver of the truck emerged from the wreckage and appeared to be okay, too.

"There were broken chicken coops strewn around on the ground and loose chickens running everywhere."

There were no stop signs, but Dad assumed that he was in the wrong and panicked!

"He just went to pieces."

Dad was sure he would be liable for the truck and lost chickens, and there was no insurance on the car. He felt certain that he would be in debt forever trying to pay for the damages. Dad and Mom walked away -- from the accident and from their beautiful car, now a mangled pile of junk lying in the ditch. They were not far from where Mom's sister, Lula, lived and headed in that direction. As they got nearer to Herman and Lula's place, Dad was in deep despair as he told Mom, "I think I'll go over the hill -- I think I'll go over the hill," over and over. After they told Herman and Lula what had happened and talked for a while, Dad settled down. In discussing what to do next, they decided the only thing to do was to find an old car they could afford and go on from there. They needed to get to their job in the potato fields. Herman gave my parents a ride home.

Later that day, Dad hitched a ride to Britt. With a heavy heart and a lingering feeling of despair, he began the task of finding another car. He ended up buying an old Chevrolet for $25.

"It was a pile of junk with no brakes and with headlights that looked like candles."

The following Sunday, after driving the old Chevy to work that week, the whole family, including Grandma Sloter, "piled in" and we headed for Herman and Lula's to show them our $25 car. On the way, a calf walked into the road in front of us. Unable to stop in time, we ran over it. Later, a pig ran into the road in front of us and we ran over it, too! The dead pig wouldn't do anybody any good lying there in the road, so Dad decided to stop and pick it up. By the time he got the old car stopped and was backing up, another car had already stopped and the driver was loading the pig into his trunk.

"Those were tough times -- everybody was in the same boat."

The authorities never did say anything about the accident with the truck, and Dad never went "over the hill". But, every now and then, Dad would talk about the Model B Ford and how much he liked that car.

SHOES

When the potato picking was finished on the Kennedy Farms near Clear Lake, Iowa, the whole crew went to work on the potato farms the Kennedy's owned near Ringsted, Iowa. Grandma Sloter was staying with us at the time, so she took care of "us kids" while Dad and Mom were gone.

The potato fields were too far from home for Mom and Dad to drive back and forth with the old Chevy. Besides, they couldn't afford the gas it would take. They would just have to sleep cramped up in the car or find a free place to stay where they could stretch out.

After locating the fields where they would be working the next day, Dad and Mom went into Ringsted to find a place to stay. By the time they decided it was hopeless, it had gotten dark. The best thing to do, they figured, was to go back to the potato field and sleep in the car. That way they would be in the field to get an early start the next day. That sounded like a good plan, but they were in unfamiliar territory and couldn't find their way back to the field. As they drove around in the dark, Dad became more and more annoyed by the situation. But it struck Mom, who had been nicknamed "Giggles" in high school, as funny.

"I got started laughing and couldn't stop. The more I laughed, the madder Bill got."

It was getting late when they finally found the field. Mom stopped giggling and Dad got over his anger. They parked the car and tried to get some sleep, Mom in the front seat and Dad cramped up in the back. They did their best to get comfortable, but it was not a restful night.

After work the next day, they drove back into town and Dad got permission for them to sleep in the train depot waiting room. There was a heating stove in the center of the room and wooden benches around the perimeter. They slept on the wooden benches, covered up with their coats.

Mom and Dad were up before daylight. It was easy for them to get up early after spending the night on wooden benches. But it was still better than sleeping in the car. Dad brought water to a boil in an old coffee can that he sat in the fire inside the heating stove. He removed it from the fire with a pair of pliers and, when it stopped boiling, stirred in some regular grind coffee. It took about three minutes for the grounds to settle and for it to be ready to drink. They enjoyed the full, rich-flavored "hobo" coffee with some bread and jelly that they had brought with them and headed for the potato field. It was still dark.

A machine was used to dig the potatoes, shake out the dirt and deposit them on top of the ground, ready to be picked up. Picking up potatoes was backbreaking work. It required constant bending over or getting down on hands and knees to gather them and put them into five-gallon wire baskets. The potatoes were then poured into gunnysacks, which held one hundred pounds. The full sacks were left standing along the rows as the workers moved across the fields. When there were no sacks available, the potatoes were poured onto the ground in piles to be "sacked" later. This created extra work so it was important to have enough sacks on hand.

They were paid 2.6 cents for each one-hundred-pound sack full they picked up. Mom and Dad were in the field picking up potatoes as soon as it was light enough to see them. They picked up three hundred and forty-five sacks of potatoes the first day and earned $9.00. That was more than a normal week's wages! It was hard work, but they were "making good money".

"The harvest season was short, so we had to 'get while getting was good'."

The other people working in the potato fields never got started as early as my parents. This proved to be a real advantage for Mom and Dad, because they were "on hand" when the potato farmer would bring the day's supply of sacks to the field.

"When Bill would see the truck coming with the sacks, he would run to it and grab as many sacks as he could carry, with some tied to his belt and the rest in his arms."

Mom and Dad would have all they needed for that day's work plus a few to start the next day. The other workers often ended up short of sacks and resented the fact that Mom and Dad always had enough. It had been the same way at Clear Lake with the same crew.

"It was 'every man for himself', but they hated us for it."

Working in the peatbeds was different from working in other types of soil in that it was much softer. Mom and Dad's shoes would sink in and fill with dirt when they would walk where the soft soil had been dug up and sifted through the potato digger. For that reason, and because the cool, soft dirt felt good on his feet, Dad liked to work barefoot. One morning, he removed his shoes and placed them on top of their first bag of potatoes at the end of the row, and left them there. At the end of the day, when Dad went back for his shoes, they were gone! Mom couldn't believe it when she heard Dad shout, "My shoes are gone! Some dirty bastard stole my shoes!"

Mom and Dad had just started the job and wouldn't be paid until the end of the week. There was no money for shoes. They needed what little they had to buy food. Finally, they went to the only dry goods store in town and asked the owner if they could have a pair of shoes on credit. But the owner wouldn't take a chance on them. Dad decided he would just go without shoes that week until payday. As it turned out, three days later, whoever took Dad's shoes put them at the end of a row where he would find them. It was good that they hadn't been able to get new ones.

MY RED COMB

It was four-thirty in the afternoon and Mom watched as my school bus came down the road, slowed down, then sped up and went on by.

Before leaving the house that morning, Mom had combed my hair as she always did before we would go to town or at bedtime. She gave me a new red comb and told me to keep my hair combed "nice" when in the schoolroom.

Mom and I stood on our driveway and waited as the school bus came rumbling down the road. When it stopped, Mom gave me a big hug. "Be a good boy," she said, as I climbed on the bus. Just as the door was closing, she added, "Don't lose your comb."

I found a seat and watched as the other kids talked and joked around like old friends. I didn't know anyone and felt alone.

It was my first day of kindergarten and I was a little apprehensive about the whole thing. After arriving at school, I was unsure of where to go, but somehow found my room. The teacher showed me where to sit. She took the "rag" rug I had brought from home, with my name pinned to it, and placed it on the shelf with the other children's "nap mats".

My troubles started at recess time that morning and got worse as the day went on. Not knowing anyone, I decided to play on the "monkey bars". Near the end of recess, I climbed up, scooted to the middle of the crossbar and hung upside down by my knees. When the bell rang signaling that recess was over, I grabbed the bar, swung down, dropped to the ground and ran to the building. When I got inside, I discovered that my new red comb was gone. My first thought was that Mom would be angry. I wanted to go back outside to look for it, but the bell had rung. I would have to look for it after school.

Later that morning, the teacher told us to get our mats down and lay them in a row on the floor and take a nap. It was nap time. That looked ridiculous to me. I was a big boy. I told the teacher that I didn't need a nap and she said to lie down and take one anyway. I stretched out on the mat, but couldn't sleep. I was thinking about my red comb and wondering if I would be able to find it.

When school let out that day, I went out of the building with all the other students, looked over at the four school busses and wondered which one was mine. I went back inside to ask the teacher. When I got back outside to board my bus, I thought, "Maybe I can find my comb first," and went to take a quick look. It wasn't under the monkey bars or in the grass around them, so I went back to get on the bus.

The buses were gone! I didn't know what to do. "Should I start walking home? It's a long way to walk. Maybe I should just sit and wait for Dad to come for me after work." I was wandering around trying to decide what to do and looking for my comb when some teachers came out of the schoolhouse and saw me. One of them came over to me and asked what I was doing there. When I told her, she said, "Stay right there," and went back inside.

I was surprised when a man, I think he was the principal, came out and asked if I knew my way home. I told him I did and he said, "Come with me, I'll take you home." We got into his car and he said, "Okay, which way?"

Corwith, Iowa, is laid out with some of the streets parallel and at right angles to the railroad track which ran at an angle through town, while others were "straight with the world", running east-west, north-south. It was confusing, especially to me when I was five.

I thought I knew the way home -- it was only about three miles north of Corwith. But I had never really needed to know before. As we left the schoolyard, I pointed left and said, "That way." As we wound our way northward out of town and approached a "T" intersection, the principal asked which way to turn and I pointed left. Just as he was ready to turn, I said, "No, turn the other way." By that time, he was beginning to doubt me and asked if I was sure I could find my way home. I told him I thought so. After making a right turn, then a left, I was sure. Soon we were driving into our yard.

Mom came running out of the house with a worried look on her face and asked what had happened. She was relieved that I was okay. Mom stood hugging me as the principal told her that I had missed the bus.

She never even asked me about my red comb.

A HOUSE OF OUR OWN

"I would look at houses with their lights on at night and think how nice it would be to have a house of our own, where nobody could push us around."

The year was 1940. Mom and Dad had been married for six years and it seemed as if we were constantly moving. It had been that way ever since Grandma Jackson had quit farming more than a year earlier. Something had to be done. The obvious solution would be to rent a house, or buy one. Renting was "ruled out" because my parents didn't like the idea of having to come up with rent money every month. And buying a house would be impossible without a down payment and a steady job. Everyone who was working for a farmer at that time was working by the month. Finally, after much discussion, Dad came up with a solution. He would build us a house! That was the most ridiculous thing Mom had ever heard, and she told him so. Dad wasn't a carpenter! Besides, how could they possibly build a house if they couldn't afford to rent or buy one? But Mom didn't know just how resourceful Dad could be.

Grandma Sloter had some money -- not a lot, but some. Dad asked her if he could borrow some money from her to build a house. She asked, "How much, and for how long?" Knowing he could count on Grandma for a small loan, Dad set out to "make it happen". He located a lot on the northwest edge of Kanawha that could be bought for $35. Then he located a large chicken house that he could have for free just for tearing it down. Mom and Dad calculated the cost for new material they would need in addition to the used lumber from the chicken house. They figured that if they used the $70 they had in savings, they could "get by" with a loan of $300. Dad would talk to Grandma again.

Grandma Sloter agreed to loan Dad and Mom the $300 they needed, and they began making preparations to build a house. Dad talked to Selmer Anderson, a retired carpenter who lived near our lot in Kanawha, and asked him to help with the construction. This satisfied Mom that the job would be done properly.

Dad tore down the chicken house, pulled the nails from the used lumber, hauled it into town and stacked it on our lot. The new lumber they needed was ordered, delivered to the lot, stacked near the road and covered. A front door and some windows were still needed. Construction was begun in the late fall of 1940, during the "off season", after the potatoes and onions were all picked up and the corn was picked.

Now it was certain, we were going to have a house of our own!

"ARMISTICE DAY STORM"

When we awoke that morning, snow had drifted across the bed where Julian, Don, and I were sleeping. Two windows had broken out in the only bedroom in the house, and there was a raging blizzard outside.

As happened with many people, the "Armistice Day Storm" of November 11, 1940 caught our family off guard. Dad was stranded in Kanawha where he was working to finish building our new house. Mom, "us kids" and Grandma Sloter were in an old two-room "farmhouse in the field" three miles north of Corwith and down a long lane. There was no electricity, no running water and no inside toilet. Our family was living there temporarily until Dad could get our new house finished enough to move into.

It was freezing cold outside and almost as cold inside. Mom stuffed some old clothes into the broken windows to keep out the cold and snow. We were all cold, but Don got so cold that his hands began to swell. Mom bundled him up in warm clothes and rubbed his hands to warm them and to get the blood circulating.

There was no fire in the cook stove and very little firewood in the house. Mom, Julian and I went through a trapdoor in the floor and down some rickety stairs into the dark, damp cellar under the house to look for something to burn. The cellar was so dark that we had to feel our way. I got down on my hands and knees and felt around on the dirt floor wondering if there were any animals hiding there out of the storm. It was creepy and a little scary for Julian and me; we were only four and five years old at the time. But Mom was with us and that gave us confidence. I found a few scraps of wood and an old shoe while Mom and Julian found some old articles of clothing. We would burn anything we could find, just to get a little heat in the house. Mom got a fire going, but we knew that what little we had to burn wouldn't last long. We needed more.

"To keep from freezing to death was the main thing."

Mom "bundled up" with several layers of clothing and tied a scarf over her face. Just her eyes showed under Dad's old winter cap. A blast of cold and snow rushed in as Mom opened the door and stepped out into the storm. Dad had left our sawhorse, buck saw and ax standing beside the house, but there was no firewood. She grabbed the saw and was soon out of sight as she headed north toward the grove of trees about twenty-five yards away.

The wind howled and the snow blew around the house as we waited for Mom to come back. We stood by the window trying to see out, but it frosted over from our breath. I got up close and blew on a spot to thaw a round, clear spot on the pane, but we still couldn't see anything through the blowing snow, and the clear spot soon frosted over. It seemed as if Mom was gone an awfully long time and we began to worry. Finally, she opened the door and stepped inside. She looked like a snowman carrying an armload of wood. Grandma said, "Oh, thank God!" and quickly grabbed some of the wood and added it to the small fire in the cook stove, just as it appeared ready to go out. Mom shook some of the snow from her clothes and moved over close to the stove. Opening the firebox door, she kneeled down and blew on the hot coals to get the fire going.

As the stove began to get warm, Mom opened the oven door to let more heat into the room. Don was still cold, so she stood him on the oven door to warm him up.

Mom took a few minutes to warm herself, then once again went outside into the storm. We needed enough firewood to keep the fire going day and night. At least now she knew where to find it. She made trip after trip to the grove, dragging logs and branches up near the house. She would saw it up later, working where the house would offer some protection from the wind.

While she was out, Mom fed the few chickens we had and gathered the eggs. She also brought water to the house, but had to pump it by hand because the wind was blowing so hard that the windmill wouldn't work.

Grandma prepared a meal for us from the food we had on hand. Mom and Dad always made sure that there was plenty to eat. There were potatoes, onions, apples, squash, canned meat and vegetables stored in the corner of the "root cellar" where we had found the few items to burn. There was also plenty of baking flour.

"We never bought bread."

I remember having freshly-baked bread and baked squash (us kids really didn't like squash but, of course, we ate it anyway), that day and fresh apples that had been picked from the trees on the farmstead that fall. Mom and Grandma had made applesauce and apple butter from some of the apples, but saved the best ones to eat fresh. Grandma showed us how to eat an apple with no waste at all. She didn't just tell us, she showed us! All that was left when we finished was the stem and seeds.

The storm raged on for three days. Mom, Julian, and I went out beside the house every day to cut wood, carry it into the house and stack it in the kitchen. By the time Dad was able to make it home on the fifth day, the kitchen was so full of wood there was barely room for anything else. Mom had made sure that we weren't going to be cold.

Dad had been safe from the storm, but conditions had not been pleasant for him either. The only place he could find to sleep was in the city jail. He was worried about his family in that old house with almost nothing to burn. But there wasn't a thing he could do for them except pray for their safety until he could get there. He was worried, but at the same time, he felt confident that Mom and Grandma could handle the situation.

It was a happy reunion when Dad finally got home and found us safe and sound. Grandma told Dad that we would not have survived if it hadn't been for Mom braving the storm to get wood for the fire. During the height of the storm, Mom had thought about trying to go to the neighbors, but she didn't think that she could make it that far.

"The neighbors even had livestock freeze to death in the pasture, because the cattle couldn't make it to the barn."

When the hugging ended and after the survival stories had been told, Dad said the house was finished enough for us to move into. It was an exciting time for us, especially Mom. We had all been looking forward to that day for a long time and could hardly believe that it had finally arrived.

Our new house was twenty-four feet wide by thirty-six feet long, and was built on posts set into the ground for a foundation. A brick chimney was built in the center of the house where the cook stove would stand. There were no inside walls, no insulation nor interior sheeting on the outside walls and no front door or windows. I guess it was more a shed than a house at that point, but it was ours and we were happy to be in it. The finish work would come later as time and money allowed.

Our house was not hooked up to city water. Dad or Mom would go to the neighbors for water that first winter, until the neighbors objected. Then we went to the fire station for water with a coaster wagon and two eight-gallon cream cans. Eventually, Dad was able to convince the city council to pipe city water to our house.

We had no toilet when we moved in. That spring, Dad built an "outhouse" using new lumber. I remember him commenting about the high cost of materials. It had cost $15 to build.

We had lived in seven different places during the previous year. Finished or not, we were happy to be moved into our own house where we wouldn't be forced to move again.

Julian, Donald and James
(On the porch of our house in Kanawha)

THE ROUGHNECK

The constant moving from place to place finally ended when we moved into our own house in Kanawha, but the struggles didn't. Dad tried many different jobs in an attempt to get ahead, rather than just make a living. There was one characteristic common to every job he tried, however. Every one involved back-breaking labor.

Soon after moving to Kanawha, Dad bought spades, shovels and a crummer. He went to work with Mom's uncle, Nels Jackson, a tile-ditch digger, to learn the trade. Before long, Dad was bidding jobs and digging tile ditches on his own.

Digging tile ditch was piece work. The more ditch (typically about eighteen inches wide and five feet deep) Dad dug, the more he earned. Weather permitting, Dad worked every day, digging as much as he could, getting stronger as he worked.

Another job Dad tried was sheep shearing. It required lifting and setting sheep and standing bent over while shearing. He developed exceptionally strong arm and back muscles in the process.

Dad was a big man, standing six-feet two-inches tall and weighing between one hundred ninety and two hundred pounds, depending on the season. His natural muscular build and the heavy work combined to make him exceptionally strong.

One time, when our family was picking up potatoes, Dad decided to demonstrate his strength after he had worked all day. Our day's work wasn't finished until we loaded all the one-hundred-pound sacks of potatoes we had picked up that day onto a flat-rack wagon. The potatoes might have frozen if left in the field overnight. When the rack came by for us to load, Dad would grab a one-hundred-pound sack of potatoes by the top of the sack and lift it about two and one-half feet off the ground and onto the rack – with one hand. I can still see the look of astonishment on the face of the man on the rack, and the crooked smile of satisfaction on Dad's face.

A LESSON

Soon after we moved into our new house in Kanawha, Mom enrolled Julian and me in kindergarten. I was five years old and Julian was four.

I had caught whooping cough soon after starting kindergarten in Corwith and missed several months of school. Thinking I would be too far behind to catch up, Mom kept me out of school the rest of the year. So, after we moved to Kanawha, she started Julian and me in kindergarten together. Although a year apart in age, we were now in the same grade.

Julian and I were the "new kids" in school. I don't recall how it began, but it happened every night after school. For some reason, a group of children from our class in Kanawha Elementary School started chasing Julian and me home after school. Other children began joining in. It became a crowd.

We told our parents what was happening and Dad's reaction surprised us. "They can't chase you if you don't run," he said. "The next time it happens, Boys, stop and face them and offer to fight. There won't be one kid in the bunch ready to fight you." There was some doubt in our minds but, if Dad said it would work, it probably would. He certainly knew more about that kind of thing than we did.

We didn't have to wait long to find out. The next Monday after school it happened again. The same group of kids ran toward us—and we ran for home. But this time it would be different. After running about a half block, I said to Julian "Okay, let's stop." He answered, "Okay," and we stopped right there and turned around, facing them with our fists up like boxers. "Okay," I said, "If you want to fight, let's fight." I can still see the look of astonishment on their faces as they stopped, stared at us for a brief moment, then turned and ran the other way. We were never bothered by them again. From then on, we felt a little more confident and were more accepted by the other children. Some of them became our friends.

MOWING LAWNS

Julian was five years old and I was six when we first heard about mowing lawns to earn money. Earning our own money sounded good to us. We discussed the idea with Mom and Dad, and they thought it would be okay for us to try. They explained that we would need to do a good job and not leave any streaks of long grass; otherwise, we wouldn't be asked back when the grass needed mowing again.

Julian and I went from door to door asking people if we could mow their lawn. Finally, after several tries, a lady on the other side of town told us that we could mow for her. She said she would pay us twenty-five cents. That sounded good to us. We had never held more than a nickel in our hand before. We agreed.

We thought she was really old. Her name was Mrs. Knudson. We called her "Mrs. Old Lady Knudson".

Mrs. Knudson had an old reel-type lawnmower. (The modern rotary mower hadn't yet been invented.) She showed us how her lawnmower should be oiled and told us that we should oil it every time we mowed. The mower pushed too hard for either Julian or me to push alone, so we 'teamed up', each taking hold of one side of the T-shaped wooden handle with both hands. We worked side by side as we pushed the mower through the grass.

Mrs. Knudson's grass was too tall for her lawnmower to cut the first time over. It was necessary for us to push the mower into the grass a few feet, pull it back, and then push it ahead again. We had to do this repeatedly to get all the grass cut to the same length. It took us a long time to finish her lawn, but we were proud of the job we had done. Mrs. Knudson invited us in for cookies and milk after we finished, and she paid us the agreed-upon quarter.

Mrs. Old Lady Knudson became a regular customer, but she would only allow us to mow her lawn once every two weeks. Her grass was always too tall. It was necessary to use the push forward, pull back, and push forward again method every time we mowed. We were aware that her lawn should be mowed more often, but we didn't want to say anything to her about it. We didn't want to risk losing her as a customer. We had other lawn-mowing jobs, but hers was the most memorable. She always invited us in for a treat of 'Kool Aid' or milk and cookies. She was a nice lady and we liked her.

Another memorable lawn-mowing job was one that lasted only one day. We solicited the job and agreed to mow the farmhouse lawn for fifty cents. That seemed about right, we thought, but we didn't realize how large it was. It was located about one hundred yards from our house. We started mowing just after noon and hadn't finished yet when suppertime came. When Dad got home from work, he came to see what was taking us so long. Taking the mower from us, he mowed the rest of the lawn. Even though we had worked all afternoon, it still took him a long time to finish. The longer Dad pushed that mower, the madder he got. By the time he finished, he was really "hot under the collar". Dad was angry because he felt that his boys were being taken advantage of, and nobody was going to take advantage of anyone in his family if he had anything to say about it. And he let the owner know it. Dad told him in no uncertain terms that would be the last time we would be mowing his lawn -- and it was.

Our neighbor, Frank Maynard, had a machine shop and sharpened reel-type lawnmowers on a special machine. He would take the mower apart and install the reel and cutting bar in the sharpening machine, sharpen them, then reassemble and adjust the mower. It was fascinating, and I watched closely as he went through each step. When finished, he would test the mower by holding a piece of paper against the cutting bar and rotating the reel to cut it. He would test and make minor adjustments over and over until the mower cut perfectly. For a final test, he would use cigarette paper. After watching Frank go through that procedure on several mowers, I began to understand how he was making the adjustments.

Sometimes our customers' mowers wouldn't cut very well, so I would use what I had learned from Frank to adjust them. It took a while for me to get the feel of it. But, eventually, I was able to make the adjustments and get the mower to cut better than it had before and to "push" easier. Sometimes it would take longer to oil and adjust the mower than Julian thought it should, and he would become impatient with me. He would complain that we could mow the lawn in the time that it took me to adjust the mower. Nevertheless, having the mower work well did make the job easier for both of us and I got satisfaction from that.

We didn't realize it at the time, but Julian and I were partners and were self-employed. We were soliciting business, negotiating our pay, contracting the jobs and striving to satisfy our customers. We both learned a lot from that experience.

A MEMORABLE CHRISTMAS

There was snow on the ground and it was a cold, but bright, sunny day in mid-December, 1941. Mom told "us kids" that we were going somewhere special. Dad and Mom loaded Don (age 3), Julian (age 5) and me (age 6), into our Model 'A' Ford and drove about forty-five miles to Ft Dodge. We seldom traveled more than a few miles from home, so that seemed like a long trip. Dad parked the car on an off street and we walked to where most of the stores were located.

There was a crowd gathering on both sides of the street. I don't recall there being many old people. It seemed like mostly people about Dad and Mom's age, and their children. We joined the crowd and waited, wondering what we were waiting for. Our parents were keeping it a surprise. We didn't know what to expect, but there was excitement in the air. Soon we heard bells jingling and strained to see what was making the sound. Finally, a team of horses came into view wearing shiny black harnesses with glittering brass bells attached. The bells were jing-jing-jingling in rhythm as the horses pranced down the street pulling a farm wagon. A man, wearing a red suit trimmed in white fur, a matching stocking cap and a wide black belt around his large middle, was riding in the back of the wagon. It was Santa Claus! We asked Mom and Dad where Santa's reindeer were and they told us that Santa had to leave his reindeer home because there wasn't enough snow. The driver stopped the horses a short distance from us and Santa began handing brown paper bags to the children. He spoke to each child and let out with a lot of HO-HO-HO's as he worked. Parents were lifting their small children up so they could get a good look at Santa and receive their bag. I wondered what was in the bags and whether there would be enough bags for all of us to get one. The horses were driven ahead a short distance at a time and finally stopped by us. It was our turn. Dad lifted Don up to receive his bag, then Santa leaned over the wagon and handed Julian and me ours. We immediately opened them and found jellybean candy, "Tootsie Rolls", hard candy and some fruit. That was exciting for us because we rarely had candy and fruit.

Receiving those bags was just the beginning of a very special day. Next, we went from store to store. Dad was looking for something, but he wouldn't say what it was.

As we walked along, we saw more Santas. I had already begun to doubt some of the stories we had heard about Santa Claus and my suspicions were confirmed that day. There were men in Santa Claus suits in two other stores and I knew they weren't the same man. I didn't want to spoil Christmas for my younger brothers, so I didn't say anything to them or to Mom and Dad.

After trying several places, Dad finally found a store that had what he wanted and he made his purchase while Mom took us kids to another part of the store. Dad had a pleased look on his face as he left the store carrying a one-foot square box wrapped in Christmas paper.

Dad had one more stop to make, one more thing to do that would make that day very special, probably as special a day for Mom as she could remember. None of us had any idea where Dad was going as we followed him down the street. A couple blocks later he walked into a jewelry store with his family trailing behind. He said to mom, "It's time you had a wedding ring -- pick one out." Mom was overwhelmed. She could hardly believe what she was hearing. Still in shock, she looked over the rings in the case and chose a plain gold band. This time there was no waiting. The jeweler measured Mom's ring finger, found the right size and handed it to Dad. He took the band and with a very pleased, crooked smile, slipped it on her finger.

Dad was ready to go home, his missions had been accomplished. Mom was a very happy lady and we kids had gotten sacks of "goodies" from Santa. But we were still very curious about what was in that box beside us in the back seat.

A Christmas tree was set up in the center of the house near the chimney (there were still very few walls separating the rooms at that time, and no inside doors) and that special box was placed under the tree. Other packages appeared as Christmas drew near, but that box held the most interest for us kids.

It seemed to take an eternity as we waited for Christmas to arrive, but Christmas Eve finally did come. When we got home after church that evening, our family gathered around the tree. There weren't many packages, but there had been fewer at other Christmases. The square box was saved until last. It wasn't very heavy, and it didn't rattle. We had no idea what it could possibly be. Julian, Don and I all worked together as we tore the wrapping paper off. We broke the tape holding the flaps of the box and lifted them up to look inside. What we saw was something that looked like brown leather balls. We still had no idea what it could be. We reached in and pulled out the soft leather objects, still wondering what they could be and what was so special about them. Finally, we realized what the gift was. It was two pairs of boxing gloves.

We tried them on and found that they were too big for our hands, and they felt heavy when we held them up like a boxer. Dad showed us how to reach inside the glove and take hold of the bead, about the size of a broomstick sewn into the center of the palm, and squeeze, making a fist. The cuffs of the gloves came halfway to Julian's and my elbows. They reached all the way up to Don's elbows. Dad laced the gloves on Julian's and my hands and we boxed our first round with them. Dad showed us how to hold our fists to protect ourselves and to punch. There wasn't much action because the gloves were so big and heavy, but we held them up as best we could and tried to punch each other.

Dad enjoyed watching Julian and me box. Later, he even took us to the "pool hall" in Kanawha and had us demonstrate our skill to the patrons. He was proud of his boys and it showed.

Those gloves provided endless hours of entertainment for us and for our friends throughout our growing-up years. They went with us as we moved back and forth across the country. They were probably the most memorable gift that we ever received from our parents. The secondary gift provided by "the gloves" was that Julian and I learned something about the art of self-defense and that gave a little boost to our self-confidence.

Dad, James (wearing boxing gloves) **and Donald**
(Our house in Kanawha.)

THE CARNIVAL

The sign at the carnival read, "Ten dollars to any man who can stay in the ring with our man for ten minutes."

To Dad, thirty-one years of age at the time, this was more than a challenge. It was an opportunity. The year was 1942 and ten dollars was a lot of money. He could earn a few days' wages in a matter of minutes.

Dad, accompanied by two of his friends, approached the "caller" at the attraction and said, "All I have to do is stay in the ring for ten minutes, right?" The caller answered, "Yeah, that's right, stay ten minutes and you get ten dollars." Now, having clarified the terms with witnesses, Dad agreed to them.

Dad was a big man and a brawler, but he wasn't stupid. He knew from the time he had spent traveling with the carnival that the man in the ring was a professional who most likely won every match. He would know "every trick in the book" and would use them. The key phrase was "stay in the ring".

The crowd cheered as Dad climbed over the ropes into the ring. They knew him and, win or lose, expected a good fight. As they watched, some of them were probably disappointed, but they were entertained and had a good laugh by the time it was over.

When the bell rang, the men came to the center of the ring – well, almost. Dad stayed his distance so the "carnie" wouldn't be able to take hold of him. Whenever his opponent would get close, Dad would quickly step aside and move to another part of the ring. After about five minutes of chasing Dad, and being unable to corner him, the fighter complained, "Why don't you stand and fight like a man?" Dad repeated the "stay ten minutes in the ring" requirement to him and continued to dodge and stay out of the carnie's reach. He stayed the ten minutes.

When asked whether he got paid, Dad said, *"Sure I got paid. If I hadn't, my friends would have taken the place apart."*

A NICKEL FOR THE MOVIES

It was early Saturday evening and Donnie, Julian and I left the house just as it was getting dark, each clutching a nickel in his little fist. We were about a block from home when Donnie dropped his money. We all got down on our hands and knees and looked in the gravel where it had fallen. Unfortunately, it was too dark to see clearly. We couldn't find it, and it was getting late. I said, "I'll run home and ask Dad for another nickel. You guys keep looking until I get back."

I ran fast because we were on our way to the Kanawha Theater to see the Saturday night movie. A cowboy movie was playing and we didn't want to be late. Roy Rogers, Gene Autry, and Hopalong Cassidy (Bill Boyd) movies were shown alternately almost every weekend. If possible, "us kids" would go to a "cowboy show" every Saturday night. It was a ritual we looked forward to.

There was never any need for our parents to be concerned about what we were seeing. The stories all had a similar theme, with the "good guys" pitted against the "bad guys". And the good guys always won. They were easy to identify because they wore white hats, while the bad guys' hats were black -- except Hopalong Cassidy, who wore all black, including his hat.

Roy Rogers, Dale Evans and Gabby Hayes, along with Roy's horse, Trigger, made a formidable team. Roy was stronger, faster and a better shot than any bad guy. Roy and his partners always succeeded in bringing the bad guys to justice. Roy's horse, Trigger, was the fastest and smartest horse in the West and could run longer than any bad guy's horse. The bad guys never stood a chance. There would always be music sometime during each movie with Roy singing alone, or along with the "Sons of the Pioneers".

Gene Autry and his sidekick, Smiley Burnette, always worked together to triumph over the evildoers, whether they were land grabbers, rustlers or someone trying to unfairly control water rights. Gene Autry, the original singing cowboy, strummed his guitar and sang in the lighter moments of his movies.

Hopalong Cassidy was a no-nonsense good guy who brought justice to bear in many different situations.

For us, these model-of-conduct movies, and the cowboys' lives, on screen and off, represented what we should strive to be.

Their movies were always thrilling, fun and wholesome. They were our heroes, our idols.

Dad gave me another nickel for Donnie, and I ran back to where Julian and Don were still looking for the lost money. We gave up the search and ran to the theater. We hurried even though we knew the feature movie wouldn't start until the "Previews of Coming Attractions" and "Newsreel" were over. But we didn't want to take a chance on missing the beginning of the movie. We sat through the previews and the "Newsreel" about what was happening on the warfront. The war news was absolutely frightening to me. I hated the tanks shooting and the planes bombing. I hated the killing and the dying. It seemed like all the news was war news. Thank goodness it was in black and white. I would have been even more frightened if it had been in color. Sometimes I would close my eyes and try not to listen.

By the time the movie was over and we had seen the cartoon, the scary news was forgotten. We left the theater with pent-up energy from sitting so long and a good feeling from the movie. We were off and running the instant we were out of the theater door, reenacting the horse chase scenes as we ran full speed for home.

A SLED OF OUR OWN

It was Winter, 1942 -- and a bright and beautiful winter day in Kanawha, the small town in north central Iowa that we had moved to from "the country" just two years earlier. There was snow on the ground and the streets were snow-packed and slippery. Julian was six years old and I was seven, and it was our second winter living in town. We watched enviously that day as the "town kids" ran carrying their sleds, flopping down on them in the middle of the street and sliding down the long hill, coasting all the way to the farm field on the edge of town. They would hurry back up the hill again for another run. It looked like so much fun, and all we could do was watch. Sure, we could go play 'Fox and Geese' in the snow, build a snowman or a fort and have snowball fights, or even run and slide on our feet, but we wanted to slide down the hill on a sled like the other kids. Right then, what they were doing looked like more fun than anything -- and all we could do was watch. We didn't have a sled.

Even though we wanted a sled more than anything, we would never have thought of asking our parents to buy one for us. We knew there wasn't any money to spare and Christmas was past. Julian and I had saved some money from mowing lawns, but not enough to buy a sled. After some discussion between the two of us, I decided that if we were going to have a sled, I would have to build one.

Dad treated our place on the edge of town as though it were a small farm. After building our house, plus a "cob house" (where we stored corncobs to burn in our kitchen stove), and a hog house and hog pen from used lumber, he had stacked the leftover lumber beside the cob house for future use. Dad allowed me to use his carpenter tools, nails and used lumber whenever I wanted to try to build something. He seemed proud that I wanted to build things, but chided me that he was never able to find his tools after I had used them. There was probably a little truth to that.

Anyway, sorting through the used lumber, I found a good three-fourths inch thick by six-inch wide board. Using Dad's hand saw, I cut off a piece about three feet long, then cut an angle at one end and rounded it off as best I could. When satisfied with its shape, I cut another board to match. These were to be the sled "runners". Next, I stood the runners on edge about eighteen inches apart and nailed boards across them. The boards were too long and stuck out

90

unevenly over the runners. After nailing the necessary boards in place, I sawed off the overhanging ends so they were flush with the runners. Next, I turned the sled upside down and nailed in some bracing to keep the runners from bending over. Using Dad's "brace and bit" (a hand operated drill), I drilled a hole in the upper front end of the runners and knotted in an old piece of rope. By this time, my project was beginning to resemble a real sled. There was one problem, however. The wood didn't slide very well on the packed snow. It needed metal on the bottom of the runners if it was going to work well. I wasn't sure of what to do about that. I walked four blocks to the local junkyard to look around. Maybe I could find something that would work. After some searching, I found a length of three-fourths-inch wide metal strapping with holes in it about six inches apart. It had been used to protect the top edges of the sides on a farm wagon box. It looked like the perfect solution. I got a little money from my Band-Aid can where I kept it hidden and bought the metal. After nailing and bending the metal into place on the bottom of the runners, I managed to cut off the excess with Dad's old, dull hacksaw.

The sled was now ready to try out. I picked it up (I couldn't believe how heavy it was!) and Julian and I headed for the sledding hill, which was just down the street from our house. I tried it out first. Lying down on the sled at the top of the hill, Julian gave me a big push and I headed down the hill. It slid quite well. Guiding it by dragging one foot or the other, I managed to stay somewhere near the middle of the road. I didn't quite reach the field that the other kids had reached, but I got to the bottom of the hill. I was elated! Julian's turn was next. The sled went a little farther that time – and it kept getting better as the day went on. We proudly took our sled to school the next day and took turns pulling each other on the way home.

Carrying that big wooden sled up the hill after sliding down was hard work, but we enjoyed using it for the rest of the winter.

I think Julian and I had more fun with that sled than we would have had with a new one. It was our own sled -- and I had built it myself!

GOING TO SEE DAD

My brother, Julian, and I are "a year-and-a-month-and-two-days apart." And that is what we used to say when someone would ask us our ages. We must have been a handful for Mom. More than once she has told us, "What one didn't think of, the other one did."

Our house in Kanawha was located on the edge of town, bordering a farm field. A drainage ditch ran north and south about one hundred fifty yards west of the house. A dirt path, wide enough for a vehicle, separated our yard from the farm field to the west. About fifty yards north of our house, a gravel road ran straight east and west.

Dad was working as a "hired man" for Bill Engh on his farm located three miles west and about a quarter mile north of Kanawha. When Dad came home at night, he would talk about what he had been doing that day. We heard about working with horses, cows and pigs, and about building fence and the various other jobs that he did around the farm. To six and seven-year-old boys, it sounded like fun!

One beautiful, hot summer day, Julian and I were playing in the yard while Mom was in the house. We started talking about how it would be fun to go see Dad at work. We were sure that if we asked Mom if we could go, the answer would be "no". So we decided to go without asking. When Mom was out of sight, we sneaked away from the back yard and ran north along the dirt path to the gravel road. Crouching in the road ditch, we ran to the bridge across the creek. After hiding by the bridge for a short time, I climbed a tree so I could see if Mom was coming, but hidden by the branches so she wouldn't be able to see me. When we were sure that we could get away without being seen, we headed west. We wore short pants, no shirt and were barefoot. When we would see cars coming, we would run down into the ditch and hide until they passed.

We hadn't gone far before the gravel on the road started hurting our feet, so we began walking on the part of the road where tires had beaten the gravel into the road or blew it off, leaving a somewhat smooth path. This felt good and we walked right along, making steady progress. But, after a while, we started noticing that the paths were hot from the sun beating on them, and it began burning our feet. Next, we walked in the grass by the side of the road where it felt soft and cool, but by then our feet were getting so tender the stubble from the mown grass hurt our feet and toes. We alternated back and forth after that, walking on the smooth paths for a while until our feet got hot, then on the grass until they were cool. We kept going! After we had walked about two miles, the sun started feeling hot on our backs. We talked about turning back, but by then we were sure we were closer to where Dad worked than we were to home. We decided to seek shade and get out of the sun for awhile. There were some evergreen trees just across the road ditch at a farm place ahead. We continued on and went down through the ditch and into the yard. It felt good in the shade under those trees, but it hurt when the pine needles on the low hanging branches touched our backs.

By this time, Mom had discovered that we were gone and was frantic with worry. She missed us soon after we left the yard, but had no idea where we had gone. Mom went to the neighbors looking for us. When she didn't find us, she asked them for help. But the neighbors couldn't help. Mom was eight months pregnant with our sister, Sandra, and also had our five-year old brother, Donald, to care for. She had no car and no telephone. She felt totally helpless and near panic.

After we got cooled down sitting in the shade, we started out again, walking west. By now we could see the Engh farm and were anxious to get there to see Dad and to get out of the sun.

We had gone only a short distance when a car came from the west and stopped. It was Dad! Mr. and Mrs. Engh had seen us when they were on their way home from town. They told Dad about seeing two boys along the road and wondered if they could be his boys. "They really looked sunburned," they said. Dad did not look pleased as he opened the back door without getting out of the car and said sternly, "Get in the car!" Dad had left work early to come get us and wasn't at all happy. We got in the back seat and noticed that it hurt when we touched the seat with our legs and back. We were severely burned! When we got home and into the house, Mom told Dad, "Don't be too hard on them -- they were coming to see you, you know." We were not punished for what we had done. Mom and Dad must have decided that the sun and the gravel road had punished us enough. When I went to bed that night, it felt like my skin was sticking to the sheet and peeling off when I moved. Mom used home remedies on our back and legs to ease the pain until we were healed.

That was the last time we tried a stunt like that! Well -- almost.

OUR PAL

Dad drove the car into the driveway that evening, got out and came into the house. Wearing a pleased-with-himself look as he unbuttoned his coat, he reached his hand inside and pulled out a little cream-colored ball of fur. He held it for a minute or so, then put it down on the floor. "It's a puppy!" we shouted, as it started to move. Dad brought us a new puppy! "What kind is it?" we asked. "It's a Heinz," Dad said. "Oh, Bill," Mom said. "We don't know what kind it is, Boys, but it looks a lot like a Chow to me." Dad took the puppy in his big hands and pried his mouth open, revealing a row of tiny white teeth. Turning the puppy's head, Dad showed us his tongue and the roof of his mouth. They were a dark, almost black color. "You can always tell a chow by looking in his mouth," he said. "It is always black. He is definitely part chow."

We had had other dogs, but they were older when we got them and, for some reason, we never seemed to have them very long. This was our first puppy. Mom said, "He'll have to be house broken and you boys will have to take care of him." "Oh, we will, we will!" we assured her.

We set a small dish of milk on the floor in front of the puppy and waited for him to drink. He just looked at it. Mom told us to push his nose into the milk so he could learn what it was. We did and some of it must have gone up his nose. He shook his head, sneezed, and licked the milk off his nose and face. But he still didn't drink. So we did it again. That time he got the idea and started lapping with his tongue, slowly at first, then eagerly as he lapped up all the milk in the dish.

Dad found a cardboard box and put an old coat in the bottom for our puppy to lie on. We put him in the box, expecting him to lie down. Instead, he looked around and jumped up the side, trying to get out. He tried several times, but eventually stopped trying and lay down. The box containing our new puppy was placed behind the kitchen stove for the night.

We all went to bed. "Us kids" went to sleep thinking about our new puppy and how much fun we would have playing with him the next day. Sometime in the middle of the night, we heard a whining, yipping sound. It kept getting louder and more persistent until it was almost constant. Soon, everyone was awake. We all got out of bed and went to the kitchen. The puppy was standing on his hind legs with his front paws on the side of the box, howling for all he was worth in his high-pitched little voice. He acted excited when he saw us. Mom said, "The puppy is lonesome, he misses his mother." She went to their bedroom, got the alarm clock and placed it in the box with the puppy. "What's that for?" I asked, "He is used to sleeping beside his mother," Mom answered. "The clock's steady tick is like his mother's heartbeat. Maybe he will settle down with the ticking clock in his box beside him to keep him company." Julian, Don and I took turns petting the puppy until finally, Mom said, "Okay, Boys, it's time to get back in bed. You can play with the puppy tomorrow." There was a little whining coming from the kitchen for a few minutes, but then all was quiet. The ticking clock seemed to work.

The next morning, Mom said, "We need a name for the puppy, Boys. What do you think we should call him?" Various names were mentioned, but when someone suggested, "Pal", we all agreed. He would be named "Pal".

Our puppy soon outgrew his box and needed to be housebroken. "Us kids" didn't know anything about that and we were in school all day, anyway. The responsibility fell on Mom. Whether it was instinct, understanding, or just wanting a clean house that made Mom good at housebreaking a dog, I don't know, but the job was done in no time. There was no fancy paper or coaxing, just Mom and her broom. When Pal was in the house, Mom would leave the kitchen door open to the outside and watch him out of the corner of her eye. When he would lift his leg or squat, Mom would grab her broom and swing at him, yelling, "You get out of here!" He would scramble for the door, slipping and sliding as he tried to get traction on the linoleum floor. Once she hit him with the broom and sent him rolling. It only took two or three times like that before he wouldn't even consider trying to "go" in the house. He was housebroken!

Pal grew into the most beloved pet any family could have. He was a companion, a playmate and a protector. When he became full-grown, he would challenge anything or anybody who appeared to him to be a threat to us. If he thought Mom was being too rough when disciplining one of "us kids", he would move between Mom and us and growl. Mom didn't like that, but she loved him for it. She had also seen Pal grab Julian's or my wrist in his mouth if it appeared that one of us was going to strike the other, or Don. He was truly our Pal.

James, Donald, Julian
Sandra
Pal

FLYING FISH

I grabbed a shovel from the cob house. Julian and I went out beside the shed and started digging. Dad had told us that we might find some worms there. It was Sunday, and Dad was going to take us fishing for the first time.

Uncle James and his family lived just a few miles from Kanawha. There was a gravel pit in an out-of-the-way place not far from their house. You had to drive up their long lane to get to it. Our cousins were about the only people who fished in that pit -- so it was like having their own private fishing hole. Dad decided to take "us kids" there and teach us how to fish.

Dad bought two "cane poles" for a quarter each, one for Julian and one for me. After tying lines to the end of each pole, Dad fastened a hook and a cork to each of the lines. We wrapped the line around the poles and hooked the hook over the bottom end of the pole to keep the line in place so it wouldn't tangle. Guiding our poles between the trees, we worked our way to the bank of the gravel pit and stood right next to the water. Dad showed us how to bait the hook by stringing a worm onto it and we were ready to catch some fish. After showing Julian and me how to swing the baited hook out beyond the end of the pole and drop it into the water, Dad instructed us on what to do next.

"Hold the pole still, Boys, let the cork sit on the water -- and be quiet, otherwise you will scare the fish," he said. "Keep an eye on the cork. Try not to talk; just sit quietly and watch. When you see the cork go under, give the pole a quick jerk to set the hook, then bring the fish in to shore. But don't jerk until you see the cork go under or you will miss the fish." Dad didn't fish; he just watched and helped us. The cork on my line jiggled a little. "Okay, Jim, you have a nibble, now watch the cork." I tensed up and watched intently. "Don't jerk yet -- wait 'til the cork goes under -- wait -- wait -- okay, jerk!" I jerked the pole upward. The pole bent in an arch -- then suddenly the cork shot up out of the water, then the rest of the line -- and then a six-inch fish! It catapulted through the air and over my head. The line struck a branch of the tree behind me and the fish spun around the branch and hung there, out of reach. About that time, Julian's cork went under. He jerked his pole upward. The same thing happened! Now, we had two fish caught up in the tree.

Dad said, "You don't have to jerk that hard, Boys – just a little jerk will set the hook." He looked at the fish hanging there for a minute or so, then climbed up into the tree and pulled down on the branches until Julian and I could grab hold of them. Then Dad climbed down and, with considerable effort, untangled our lines and fish.

With the fish finally on the ground, Dad showed us how to take hold of a bullhead so that the "stingers" sticking out on each side behind their gills wouldn't stick us. He also showed us how to remove the hook from the fish's mouth. Having each caught a fish, we could hardly wait to get our lines back into the water.

We caught several more fish that day, including a few more "flying fish". It seemed that every time the cork went under, we found it difficult to "hold back" and not jerk too hard. Dad cleaned the fish when we got home and we had fresh bullheads for supper. We also had some good laughs over our catching "flying fish".

A TREAT FOR MOM

Having enjoyed the success of our lawn-mowing business in the summer, Julian and I were looking for a way to earn money in the winter. It was probably only natural that we turned to shoveling snow. We knew of no other opportunities for someone our age in the small town of Kanawha.

We had always worked together and had split our earnings when mowing lawns, so it was natural for us to do the same when "shoveling sidewalks". Even though I was a year older than Julian, there was never any thought about whether one of us was doing more or less than the other. We each worked as hard as we could and knew the other was doing the same. In fact, we often worked harder than we might have otherwise, because we knew the other was also working hard.

Mrs. Old Lady Knudson was a valued lawn-mowing customer -- and she was our best sidewalk customer, as well. She would always invite us in for cookies and hot chocolate when we finished, or sometimes before when the snow was deep. We were always happy to see it snow, especially when school was let out because of it. And we could always count on shoveling for Mrs. Knudson, and would go there first.

One cold, winter day when school had been cancelled, Julian and I finished Mrs. Knudson's sidewalk, had our hot chocolate, collected our pay and headed for home. It was very cold, so when we got to Main Street, we stopped at Johnson's Drug Store to warm up. While there, we got the idea of buying a treat for Mom and decided on a vanilla ice cream cone. The cone cost a nickel, so that left twenty cents for us to divide. It would be a nice treat, and there wouldn't be any danger of having it melt before we got home!

One of us took a mitten off and carried the cone with a bare hand. In an attempt to keep our hands from getting too cold, we took turns carrying the cone as we ran for home. Our hands and fingers got really cold, anyway. Julian carried it the last block or so and his fingers were almost frozen when we finally got home and entered the house.

Mom was surprised. "Oh, Boys, you shouldn't have done that," she said. But I could tell she was pleased. She gave us each a big hug and a kiss on the cheek, and said, "You are so cold!" The look on her face, as she helped us to remove our coats and as she rubbed our hands to warm them, made me think she might start to cry. Us, too!

"I couldn't believe you two did that."

THE PROVIDER

Dad eased the car to a stop on the deserted gravel road west of town and rolled down the window. After looking over a hole in the snow, located in the ditch near the fence, I watched from the back seat as he quietly and carefully pointed the barrel of his twenty-two-caliber rifle through the open window. Steadying the rifle on the door, he took careful aim at a spot off to one side of the hole in the snow and squeezed the trigger. The rifle cracked and a cottontail rabbit convulsed up through the snow, jerked for a few seconds, then lie still.

The winters got long for Dad. He always had work in the spring, summer and fall, but when farm field work was done for the year, he was out of a job. The winters dragged on, but Dad seemed to enjoy the "free time", too. He was a gifted scrounger and used that gift to provide for his family. Dad enjoyed hunting and often used that means to provide meat for the table, supplementing and adding variety to the food that had been canned and preserved the previous summer.

Road hunting was a "lazy man's way" of hunting, but very effective. Dad had studied rabbit shelters. He knew how a rabbit would dig down through the snow and into the grass or brush under the snow to create a den. He also seemed to know which direction and how far back away from the hole the rabbit was likely to be. He became very skilled at shooting into the snow near a rabbit hole and hitting a rabbit.

Pheasants, the other game that frequently provided meat for our table, were hunted at the same time and in much the same way. They could be found hovering in the grass or brush along the road ditches and in groves of trees around farm places. There was no controlled season for hunting rabbits, but there was for pheasants. Dad ignored the seasons and hunted whenever there was a need. The authorities ignored Dad. I'm sure they knew that Dad was providing food for his family.

Hunting game was but one way that Dad provided meat for the family. Farmers who hired Dad often had "runt" pigs that would do poorly if left with the larger, healthier pigs. Rather than leave the runts in the pen with the other pigs, or move them to some other location and give them special care -- or just kill them -- they would give them to Dad. Dad was always happy to "help them out".

Dad built a small hog house and pen beside the cob house at the southwest corner of our lot. This made it possible for him to raise a runt pig or two whenever they were given to him. Food scraps given to Dad by local restaurants provided most of the feed for the pigs. He bought mineral supplements to help them along and they always thrived.

On more than one occasion, Dad was given pigs that had ruptures. If they had a stomach rupture, Dad would lay them on their back in a wood feed trough in the hog pen, tie them down and operate on them right there. Kerosene or turpentine was used as disinfectants. If a pig were ruptured in the rear, Dad would hang the pig up by its hind legs to do the operation. His methods were crude but, to my knowledge, he never lost a pig.

Old boars would bring almost nothing on the market. Their meat had a pungent, unpleasant smell when cooked. For that reason, on one occasion a farmer gave Dad a boar that was no longer of use to him. He was huge! Dad didn't want to butcher a boar and have meat that would smell bad when cooked any more than anyone else would. The only solution was to castrate him. When small pigs are castrated, they take it pretty much in stride and heal quickly. That is not the case with a full-grown boar. They often become very sick and there is a far greater risk of infection. Flies bother them, too. They sometimes die from the operation.

Dad tied a rope around the boar's snout, and tied his feet together in the pen behind our house. That was no easy task. The huge animal didn't care one bit for the idea and fought a terrific fight, but Dad finally got him "hog-tied". Dad put a keen edge on his knife, disinfected the area with kerosene and went to work. The boar got very sick after the operation and just laid around for several days. Flies swarmed around the wound. Dad instructed Mom to pour kerosene on the area to keep the flies off while he was at work.

"I was so worried about that thing dying. But he pulled through."

After about three months, the boar's system had a chance to clear out and Dad butchered him. The meat tasted great and there was no "boar" odor at all when it was cooked. That huge animal provided meat for a long time.

There was, for a time, a stray goat roaming the streets of Kanawha. We would see him every so often in different parts of town. One day, Dad came home with a bunch of fresh meat. Dad told us a farmer had given him a crippled calf to butcher. Aunt Gladys and some friends were invited for a meal that evening. When the meal was over, Dad asked, "What did you think of the meat?" After everyone said it was good, he confessed that it was goat meat. Aunt Gladys wasn't very happy about the deception, but she got over it. Over the next few days, "us kids" noticed that the stray goat wasn't around anymore. I became suspicious that we were eating that stray goat, but never said anything. I wasn't sure.

Dad would bargain, or barter, whenever he could to improve on a situation. He got a job tiling for Ralph Ludeke on his farm near Clear Lake, Iowa. When it came time to settle up, Mr. Ludeke told Dad that he was short of cash.

"Everybody was short of cash. It was hard times."

Mr. Ludeke asked Dad if he would take a butcher hog as payment. Dad agreed and was told to pick out the one he wanted and put it in his car. Dad opened the car door, then stepped over the fence into the hog pen. Ralph could hardly believe what he was seeing as he watched Dad make his way to the largest hog in the pen, bend down, reach his arms around the hog's middle, lock his hands together, and lift the two-hundred-pound animal off the ground! Ralph opened the gate for Dad as he carried the hog, kicking and squealing, to the car and put it inside. Ralph Ludeke was amazed and amused. Dad had made a good trade!

The following year, Dad did tiling for Ralph Ludeke again. This time, when it came time to settle up, Dad told Mr. Ludeke he would like to have a cow as payment. He agreed to the bargain and told Dad to pick out a cow. Having had considerable experience with dairy cows when he worked as a hired man on the farm, Dad had special insight into what to look for in a milk cow. He chose a nice little Guernsey and hauled her home in a trailer that he borrowed from Mr. Ludeke.

At first, we didn't have a place for her. She was simply milked morning and night wherever she happened to be standing. Mom could just walk up to her and say, "So boss," and she would stand still while Mom milked her.

"She was the best damn cow I ever saw in my life."

During the day, we "staked her out" along the road ditch, which provided free pasture. That fall, Dad built a small, one-stall barn for our cow. There was room for her and also room enough to store the necessary grain, hay and bedding.

The milk, butter and cottage cheese produced by that little Guernsey made getting her one of the best deals Dad ever made. Our family had difficulty consuming all that she produced, and we didn't always have pigs around to consume the excess milk. Mom didn't want to waste anything, so she tried to be creative. One dish that Mom made, in order to use as much of the milk as possible, was called "gloat". She heated milk in a pan and stirred in flour to thicken it. Hot gloat had the consistency of pudding. It was spooned onto a plate and marked with a knife as in cutting a pie. A chunk of butter placed in the middle would melt and run along the groves formed by the knife. Mom would then sprinkle it with cinnamon and sugar. At first, it didn't taste bad. In fact, we liked it. But we all got really tired of it after awhile.

We also consumed a lot of very rich homemade ice cream. Mom used only cream in a recipe that called for more than half milk.

We churned butter by placing one and one-half quarts of properly-aged cream into a two-quart fruit jar and shaking it by hand until it separated into butter and buttermilk. Mom would then take the butter from the jar, add a little salt, and press it with a spoon to squeeze out all of the buttermilk.

Mom also made cottage cheese.

One way or another, Dad and Mom always managed to provide plenty of food for the family.

A WHEELBARROW

Dad built a one-stall barn on the back of our lot in town for our Guernsey cow. The cow's stall was cleaned out once a day in the winter. The manure was pitched outside in a pile to be moved in the spring. When spring would come, Dad would tell us kids to carry the manure to our garden and spread it out before the garden was spaded. It wasn't a long way from the barn to the garden, but we thought it was too far to carry that pile of manure one forkful at a time. Dad gave Julian and me the job to do, but it was up to us to figure out how best to do it. Julian was seven years old and I was eight. There had to be an easier way than carrying it all by hand one pitchfork at a time. If only we had a wheelbarrow. I had built a sled -- I should be able to build a wheelbarrow, too. Julian thought it was a good idea – or at least he said so. But maybe he was just happy to put off spreading manure for awhile! In any case, a wheelbarrow would have other uses, as well. I decided to give it a try.

I had some idea of what a wheelbarrow should look like. Raiding Dad's lumber pile once again, I found some wood that could be used for the project. Now, all I needed was a wheel and an axle. There was nothing like that around our place, and buying a new one was out of the question. I once again raided my Band-Aid box. I always managed to keep a little money in my special hiding place by selling scrap metal that I found at the local dump, by mowing lawns, shoveling sidewalks and collecting pop bottles. With money in hand, I headed for my favorite supply place, the local junkyard.

After considerable searching, I came up with an old steel wheel about a foot in diameter – also, an old carriage bolt and several large washers that would work as an axle. By this time, the people at the junkyard were getting to know me. Not only had I bought the metal for my sled runners from them, but also they were the people to whom I had been selling scrap aluminum and copper. They charged me very little for the wheel and bolt. Dad had everything else that I needed to complete the project. I cut rails (which also served as the handles), and decking and stands, designing and building as I went. Eventually, we ended up with a very crude-looking, but functional, wheelbarrow.

As planned, the first thing we used the wheelbarrow for was to haul manure to the garden. It was fun to get good use out of something I had personally built. I was beginning to learn how satisfying it could be to create things with my own two hands.

Dad and Mom didn't say much about the project, but I could tell that they approved – and were pretty impressed.

WHEN DAD WAS AWAY

There were times when Dad was forced to travel away from home to find work. One such time was when he went to "The Dakotas" to build ammunition storage shelters for the government. Hundreds of these concrete, igloo-shaped structures were built in desolate areas of our country, which included parts of North Dakota and South Dakota. They were used during World War II to store munitions for the war effort.

Another war-effort project in which Dad was involved was construction of a prisoner-of-war camp just west of Algona, Iowa, in 1942. It was built to imprison German SS officers. The camp's location in the center of the United States made escape -- and the prisoners' potential return to the battlefield -- nearly impossible.

When Dad was away, Mom was left with the total responsibility of maintaining our household, which included caring for "us kids", milking the cow and whatever else needed doing, as well as "working out" doing housework for two other families. On top of all that, Mom decided to take in washing and ironing! She charged one dollar per basket -- that is, she would wash and iron a basket full of clothes for just one dollar. This she did "on her own", without Dad knowing about it. Mom's eighteen-cent-an-hour cleaning jobs were extremely low pay, but what she charged for washing and ironing was even worse. Mom knew she was working too cheaply, but we needed the money.

When Dad returned home after his job in the Dakotas was finished, he was pleased with how well Mom had managed while he was gone. But, at the same time, he was upset by the fact that she had been taking in washing and ironing for such a low price. He felt that someone was taking unfair advantage of her. Mom had a basket of clean and pressed clothes ready to be picked up. Dad asked Mom whose clothes they were and where they lived. Saying he would deliver them, he grabbed the basket and headed out the door. He wanted to talk to the owners face-to-face. Dad collected the dollar, but made it clear that Mom would not be doing any more of their washing and ironing. No one was going to take advantage of his wife or anyone else in his family if he had anything to say about it. Mom continued to take in washing and ironing, but she got paid more for it after Dad got involved.

"FRESH" ORANGES

We always had enough to eat at our house, but one thing we didn't have much of was fresh citrus fruit. It took money to buy citrus fruit and money was always in short supply.

Fresh oranges and grapefruit were furnished to needy families by the county, but my parents weren't about to ask for help -- especially since papers denying our family help from the county had been served on us when we moved into Hancock County.

Our next door neighbors in Kanawha did receive help, however, and were given many commodities, including oranges and grapefruit. One cold winter day a truck pulled up to our neighbor's house. The driver carried boxes of food commodities into their house as we watched from our kitchen window. They sorted the fruit and threw three spoiled oranges into the snow-bank in our front yard. Mom told me to run and get those discarded oranges out of the snow. She cut away the spoiled spots before pealing and dividing the oranges for us kids. The oranges tasted good, but on that day I gained a real sense of what it felt like to be "poor".

THE SALE BARN

There were no organized activities (at least, none that we knew of) for kids our age in Kanawha, Iowa, in the 1940's. But that didn't keep us from having fun. In fact, I believe that many of the things we found to occupy ourselves during those early years were more fun than organized activities would have been.

For one thing, there was a livestock auction every week in the sale barn across town. Even though we were "town kids", we found it interesting. Julian and I (ages five and six) and a friend went there quite often. The sale barn had areas where the livestock was penned up until it was time for them to be auctioned off. It was interesting to watch as the various gates would be opened and the livestock moved through alleyways to the auction ring, then out of the ring and back to the pen by another way. But the best place to play was where the bales of hay for the animals were stored in stacks. The bales were 1 1/2' X 1 1/2' X 4', held together with "bailing wire". With great effort, we could lift the bails and move them around to create secret passages that we could crawl through, and sometimes even walk through in a crouched position. We stacked some of the bales, leaving two-inch gaps where we could look out, yet not be seen. We let our imaginations soar while we waited for the auctions to begin. We played "cops and robbers", "cowboys and Indians", and knights sneaking through secret passages in a castle.

The hay storage area was located next to the auction ring, just behind the bench where the auctioneers and clerk sat facing the ring and facing the farmers who were there to buy livestock. There was an area behind and above the auctioneer's bench where we could lean over and watch the auction, and where we listened with fascination to the lilting chant of the auctioneers. That was an innocent enough activity, but then one of us noticed that the auctioneer and clerk's wide-brimmed hats were shaped to create a "cup" in the crown. That led to the idea of throwing paper wads in an attempt to land them in the hats. We wadded up paper balls about the size of small marbles or pencil erasers and tossed them at our targets. We tested our skill, oblivious to the people watching the auction. Some of the paper wads would land on target. Some would strike the rim of the hats and others would miss entirely. I'm sure everyone in the audience could see us, and some no doubt did. The men wearing the targeted hats either didn't notice what was happening, or just chose to ignore it. We felt daring and were prepared, if necessary, to make a quick exit and hide in the tunnels that we had constructed in the hay behind us.

Our trips to the sale barn on auction day were always fun and entertaining as we used our imaginations to create our own amusement.

THE "CRICK"

The "crick" west of our house provided endless hours of entertainment for Julian and me, and for our friends, Ray Maynard and 'Buzz' Diabler. One of our favorite pastimes was to cut fallen trees along the crick bank into lengths suitable for building a raft. We worked on the raft project for countless hours, planning to build two rafts so we could play pirates. The building project ended up taking so long that we only built one raft, so the pirate games never took place. But it was fun being "pioneers" as we crossed the big rivers on our way West.

The crick was deep enough to float our raft, but too shallow to "swim" in – except for one place about one hundred or so yards north of the bridge northwest of our house. On hot days when we wanted to cool off, we would head for the crick in short pants. The water looked dirty and the soft mud bottom oozed between our toes. Those unappealing elements made swimming there somewhat repulsive, but the worst part was the "bloodsuckers" (leaches). The crick was loaded with them. When we would get out of the water, we would always find several on our feet, toes and ankles. We would immediately sit down on the bank and try to remove them. They were too slippery to grab hold of, so we usually ended up scraping them off with a stick or sharp rock. We really hated those slimy, revolting little creatures and eventually stopped swimming in the crick because of them.

The crick also provided entertainment for us in the winter. We didn't have ice skates, but we liked to play on the ice anyway. Julian and I would take turns pulling Don on the sled I built, or just run until we got up enough speed to slide a ways.

Knowing that we would eventually get cold from playing on the ice, we would sometimes take matches along to build a fire. Dad was aware of what we were doing, but he didn't forbid it. All he said was, "Be careful, Boys, so you don't catch a cornfield on fire. It would take me the rest of my life to pay for it."

One wintry Sunday afternoon, Julian and I took Don with us to play on the crick. I was seven, Julian six and Don four. As usual, after we started to get cold, we built a fire in the middle of the crick. Somehow, our fire spread to the dry grass on the ditch bank and quickly up over the bank into the cornfield. Julian and I fought the fire by stomping on it at first, but that did little good. We then used our coats to try to beat it out, but it was spreading too fast. We were losing ground. The fire kept getting farther and farther ahead of us. Finally, I told Julian to run and get Dad while I stayed to fight the blaze. Don was too small to be of much help, but he tried to stomp out the small blazes. We were in the area of the swimming hole, so we were about two hundred and fifty yards from the house. Julian took off running at full speed. I was in near panic as I fought the fire with all I had. Soon Julian and Dad were beside me fighting the blaze with gunnysacks that Dad had brought from home. Dad didn't say much, he just went after the fire with fury, swinging the gunnysack and stomping to put it out. It made a tremendous difference with Dad there to help. Finally, the fire was out. After checking to be sure there were no sparks anywhere, we walked toward home, exhausted. There was no lecture from Dad, and no discipline of any kind. All he said was, "I think you have learned a good lesson today, Boys."

I didn't realize until years later that there was no risk of financial loss in that cornfield fire. The corn had already been picked. However, the fire could have spread to the farm buildings if it hadn't been stopped. That was the last fire we ever built along the crick.

THE CAR TRUNK

We propped the 1935 Ford car trunk open about an inch. Peering through the opening, we were able to see just a little out behind as Dad drove down the highway.

Torn between the desire to be "on his own" and to have a steady job, Dad began reading help-wanted ads in the paper. A dairy farmer near Hubbard, Iowa, was advertising for a fulltime man with experience to manage his dairy herd. Mom and Dad talked it over and decided that Dad should "check it out". Having overheard our parents talking about it, "us kids" were curious and anxious to know what was going to happen.

I wanted to go along with Dad, but he said "no". I really wanted to see the farm and hear what the farmer had to say. But when Dad said, "No," he *meant* "no". I came up with the idea of getting into the trunk without being seen so I could go anyway. That way, I may be able to hear what Dad and the farmer were saying and I would probably be able to see some of the farm from the trunk. I didn't want to go alone, so I asked Julian to go with me. Showing what I now see as better judgement, he refused. I asked Don to go, and he agreed. Don was no doubt curious, too – and, at age four, he didn't know any better than to listen to his big brother.

The trunk on a 1935 Ford wasn't very large, but large enough for two small boys. While Dad was in the house getting ready to go, Don and I climbed into the trunk and closed the lid. The latch on the trunk didn't latch automatically; it could only be fastened shut from the outside. We would be able to get out if we needed to.

After Dad started down the road, we propped the trunk open just a little to be sure we would get enough air. We rode there without making any noise while Dad headed toward Hubbard, about eighty miles southeast of Kanawha. We had been riding for what seemed like a long time when Dad stopped the car and got out. We watched through the small gap in the trunk lid as he walked across the parking lot and into a restaurant. Don and I sat all scrunched up in the small trunk, talking and waiting for Dad to return to the car. We watched as he came out of the restaurant and walked toward the car. He looked toward the trunk, but we never thought anything about that, we were sure Dad wouldn't notice that the lid was open a crack. He did notice though. He also saw the tops of our heads, slightly visible through the opening. "I thought someone had put a dog in my trunk," he would say later. Anyway, he walked right up to the trunk and opened it. There we were. We had been caught! Dad ushered us out of the trunk and into the back seat of the car. He looked and sounded really angry. We were too far from home for Dad to turn back, so he continued on toward Hubbard, reaching toward the back seat every now and then with his right hand as if he was trying to hit us. I was convinced then, as I am now, that if he had really wanted to hit us, he could have. He wanted to teach us (mainly me) a lesson without striking us.

We hadn't been gone long when Mom asked Julian where Don and I were. After he told her, she worried whether we would be all right in the trunk of the car. But there was nothing she could do except wait until we got home to see how we had gotten along.

By the time we reached our destination, Dad had "cooled down" and even let us out of the car while he talked to the dairy farmer. We heard about how close we would be to school, about a swimming hole in Honey Creek not too far from the farm place, and how good the working conditions would be for Dad.

The ride home wasn't all that pleasant, but not unpleasant either. Dad just didn't say much. I suppose he was deep in thought about what he had seen and felt there on the dairy farm. After we got home, the conversation about the farm was short. For reasons that Dad didn't discuss, taking that job was out of the question.

We never heard much about what Don and I had done, either. The whole matter was closed.

A "BB" GUN

As I walked home from town, I took a shortcut through an alley a short distance from our house. There, in a junk barrel, ready to be taken to the dump, was a BB gun -- a Red Ryder Daisy BB gun. I was seven years old and had been wishing that I had one. I had never told Mom and Dad, because I was sure they couldn't afford it. It would have been selfish of me to ask.

I took the Daisy Air Rifle from the junk and looked it over. There was nothing broken on the outside and it looked good. I thought maybe it would work and, if it didn't, maybe Dad could "fix it" for me. Filled with excitement and anticipation, I ran for home carrying my new possession.

Dad wasn't home. Impatient to try it out, I took the gun barrel in my right hand and the cocking lever in my left hand and pulled as hard as I could on the lever. I couldn't even begin to cock it. Not ready to give up, I placed the end of the gun barrel on the bottom step of our wood porch and pulled down on the lever with both hands. That time, it came about half way, but I couldn't pull it far enough to catch. Still determined, I got myself into a better position by moving the barrel up one step and, using all my strength, pulled down on the handle again. That time, it worked! I got it cocked.

I could hear a couple BBs rolling around as I tipped the gun back and forth. Knowing that it had BBs in it, I pointed the gun at the wooden step and pulled the trigger. The gun fired, but nothing came out. I struggled to cock it again and pulled the trigger, still nothing. There was definitely something wrong with it.

Examining the gun, I saw what looked like a bottle cap with a hole in it where the BBs should come out screwed on the end of the barrel. It appeared to be made to screw off. I tried with my hand, but it wouldn't move. Then, I tried it with a pair of pliers. That time it came loose. I unscrewed the cap and removed it along with a tube that was part of it. As I examined the piece, the cause of the problem became evident. There were two BBs lodged in the catch funnel on the side of the tube and nothing could get past. Using a piece of wire, I managed to dislodge the stuck BBs.

Again, taking some of my lawn-mowing money that I had saved in the old metal Band-Aid can, I went uptown to the hardware store and bought a round paper container filled with one hundred BBs. It cost a nickel. I was ready to try out my "new" gun.

I opened the end of the barrel again and poured in the BBs. Cocking the gun, I pointed it at the step and fired. That time, a BB came out and made a dent in the wood. It worked! Elated, I tried it again, and it worked the second time.

I ran into the house and told Mom about my good fortune -- of finding the BB gun in the trash and making it work. All she said was, "Be careful, Jim" and, "Don't shoot your eye out." Undaunted, I could hardly wait to tell Dad. I had a BB gun and had been able to fix it all by myself!

IT'S A GIRL

I was eight years old and probably should have noticed, but I didn't. I had brought a friend home with me to play when I found out on that Saturday in March. We were playing in the yard and Mom came outside. After Mom went back into the house, my friend said, "Your mother is going to have a baby." I couldn't believe it at first, but after he said that, I could see it was true. I hadn't noticed or paid any attention to Mom's expanding waistline before that. It must have been because it had developed gradually.

As the summer progressed, the fact became more and more evident. One hot summer day in July, Dad took Julian, Don and me to a neighbor's house and left us there. He called Dr. Wally in Corwith to come and told him how to find our house in Kanawha. The doctor told Dad, "I will leave right away. I don't want to be too late like I was the last time you called me, when Julian was born." He got to our house in time and delivered a healthy baby girl. Sandra Kay Sloter was born in the afternoon on July 27, 1943.

Dad was elated to get a girl. Julian, Don and I were also happy to have a new baby sister. In fact, we were so excited about her that the next day the three of us were hanging over the side of her crib to get a good look at her and tipped the crib over. She ended up on the floor with the mattress and bedding on top of her. We were really afraid that she would be hurt. As Mom worked to get Sandra out from under the mattress, Julian and I ran uptown and told Dad what had happened. He rushed home with us to see if his baby girl was okay. She was, of course, and we all breathed a sigh of relief. After that, we all helped care for our little sister any way we could, but were careful not to tip the crib over again. She was a precious addition to our family.

REALITY

Yakima, Washington -- 1944

The kid sitting across from me in the classroom leaned over in my direction, pointed to a word in the geography book and asked, "What does that say?" It was the word "island" and he didn't expect me to be able to pronounce it correctly.

Our first personal contact in the Yakima Valley was with Herman Rayfield's brother-in-law, Howard Dykes. The Dykes family welcomed us into their home where we stayed for a few days until we found a house to rent. They didn't have much room, so we slept on the floor using bedclothes that we had along.

Needing a place to live right away left my parents little choice but to take the first house that came along. Mr. Dykes knew of a vacant two-room house in the country, west of Yakima, close to where they lived. It was available -- and was cheap -- so we moved in. Mom and Dad took the bedroom and "us kids" slept in the large room that served as a kitchen, dining room, living room and bedroom. The floors were bare six-inch-wide boards with gaps between. There was no paint anywhere, inside or out. The yard was rocks and dirt, with no grass. An "outhouse" stood about fifty feet east of the house. We didn't feel at all good about being in that place. The humble little house we left in Iowa was far nicer.

Dad needed to start earning some money so, with Howard Dykes' help, he got a job pruning fruit trees in a nearby orchard. The next priority was to find a decent place to live. Dad began looking for a house to rent in Yakima.

There was no way of knowing how long we would live in the country, so Julian and I started school. We could either walk about three miles to school on the gravel road or go about half as far by taking a "shortcut" over a couple fences, through a field and over a large hill. After trying both ways, we usually took the shortcut. The schoolhouse had one room and one teacher, who taught several grades. It was an unpretentious country setting, but they were "way ahead" of what we had been studying in the fourth grade in Iowa. We did poorly in all classes. To our classmates, we were "the stupid kids from Iowa". No one befriended us. It was a lonely, disheartening time. Our parents were aware of what was happening and tried to compensate. They even bought us new shoes to wear to school. I was proud of my new "engineer boots", but that really didn't change things.

After one month "in the country", Dad found a house on the outskirts of Yakima at North Forth and "O" Street. Fourth Street ran north to the Yakima River, which separated the city from the mountains to the north and east. Graveled "O" Street teed off Fourth Street near its north end and dead-ended at an irrigation ditch two blocks west. The house we rented was on the south side of the street , a block west of Fourth Street. Our landlords, Rudy and Vi Pieti, lived up the hill next to the irrigation ditch. There were two other small rental houses between our house and theirs.

The house wasn't anything to get excited about, but it had a separate kitchen, dining/living room and a lean-to bedroom. The bedroom was just large enough for two double beds with a two-foot walkway between them. The bedroom contained one small, thirty-inch wide by eighteen-inch high slide-by window centered on the west wall between the beds. The room was entered through an open doorway from the dining/living room. Julian, Donald and I slept in one bed and Mom and Dad slept in the other. Sandy slept on the couch in the dining/living room.

The dining/living room had a table that we could all sit around. We used apple boxes for chairs. A couch was the only other piece of furniture in the room. Most of our clothes and other personal belongings were stored in cardboard boxes stacked along the walls around the room.

The kitchen was south of the dining/living room. It could be entered through an open doorway between the two rooms and from an outside porch to the west. It had a wood-burning stove which was used for cooking and which was also the only source of heat in the house. There was a small table and a freestanding cupboard, with a pull-out counter, sitting in one corner.

Our firewood consisted of the bark-covered, rounded sections cut from logs and rejected lumber from the nearby sawmill. It was cut into sixteen-inch lengths and delivered by the truckload. We stored the wood out of the weather under a ten-foot-by-twenty-foot steel-roof shelter south of the house. Julian and I were responsible for stacking it away under the roof and later for splitting and taking it into the house, as needed.

A small chicken house with a fenced-in area was located about twelve feet west of the wood shelter. An "outhouse" stood south of the wood shelter. Our car was parked in the back yard between the house and the other buildings. There was no lawn, only rocks and dirt. We were in desert country and nothing would grow without being watered.

This was to be home for the next three years.

Julian and I weren't looking forward to enrolling in another new school, especially in a city of thirty-six thousand people! The population of Kanawha, Iowa, was less than five hundred. For that reason, and because of all that had happened to us in the country school, we were very apprehensive about what might happen next. If the country school was that much ahead of us, what would the city school be like? Julian and I went to Lincoln School the day after moving into Yakima and stood in front of the fourth-grade teacher's desk feeling very vulnerable. After finding out the basics about us, our new teacher asked us for our grades from the previous school. We were sure we would fail if she knew the grades we got in the country school. "We didn't bring them," I told her. I then asked her if she would take the grades we would get from then on to determine what our previous grades should have been. She surprised us by agreeing to the proposal. We had a chance!

Julian and I struggled through the last few months of school, managing to get passing grades. We finished the fourth grade at Lincoln School in the spring of 1944. School was finally out! It was with a profound feeling of relief that we left Lincoln School, secure in the knowledge that we would advance to fifth grade at nearby Barge School in the fall.

FRUIT HARVEST

THE FIRST DAY

CHERRY HILL -- 1944

We had never seen anything like it! It was beautiful! The twenty-foot-tall tree was absolutely hanging full of fruit. The cherries hung touching each other on their two-inch-long stems, forming large clusters near the ends of the branches, thinning out farther up. We called it "hanging in ropes". The lower branches bent down, almost touching the ground, from the weight of the fruit.

Dad pruned fruit trees while waiting for the cherry-picking season to begin. Finally, the day we were all anxiously awaiting arrived. Our landlady, Viola Pieti, was hired to take care of Sandy. Dad, Mom, Julian, Don and I drove about forty miles south of Yakima to "Cherry Hill", near Sunnyside, and our first cherry-picking job. The cherry farmer for whom we were going to work was George Oliver. We were there bright and early, ready to get started.

Each of us, except Don, was issued a harness, a ladder and a hook. Don was only five and not old enough to pick. (Julian was eight years of age and I was nine.) We were also furnished with about a dozen twelve-quart pails.

The harness was made of two-inch-wide straps sewn together and worn much like suspenders. Hooks at the ends were clipped into holes in the rims of the pails. The straps could be adjusted to hold the pail about waist high.

The hooks were 3/16-inch steel rods about four feet long with a hook at each end. They looked a lot like the hooks we had used to catch chickens at home in Iowa. But these were used to reach up and pull down the out-of-reach branches. The branches were hooked just above the cluster of fruit with the narrow end while the other end was hooked to the side of the ladder. This would bring the cherries within easy reach and free up both hands for picking. Most of the picking was done while standing "backwards" on the ladder, facing the branches.

The most commonly used ten-foot-tall to sixteen-foot-tall ladders were "three legged", which allowed them to stand firmly on uneven ground. The bottom steps were about four feet wide, while the higher steps got progressively narrower to about a foot wide at the top of the ladder. The wide-spread legs at the bottom gave the ladder sideways stability. The slightly shorter third leg was a two-inch-by-two-inch pole, hinged at the top step.

Sometimes when a very tall tree was being picked, a "spike" ladder was used. The name was appropriate because it looked much like a large nail. The ladder was long and narrow with the sides extending past the top step, coming almost together in a point. This type ladder was set with the top straddling a branch high up in the tree. A piece of rope was used to tie the ladder in place to prevent it from slipping. With the ladder fastened in such a way, a person felt reasonably safe, even though high up in a tree; at least the ladder wasn't going anywhere.

Our family had two ten-foot ladders, a twelve-foot ladder and a sixteen-foot ladder when we started that first day. Dad did a lot of ladder-setting at first, until the rest of us "got the hang of it".

To set a ladder, it had to be positioned standing straight up close to the tree where there was an opening between branches. Good pruning provided those openings. While holding the ladder with one hand, the leg would be pushed out from the ladder toward the trunk of the tree with the other hand. At the same time, the top of the ladder was allowed to tip toward the tree until the leg touched the ground. If done properly, the ladder would then be positioned under branches where they could be easily reached. Mom, Julian and I were small, so handling the ladders was difficult for us. We helped each other as much as possible so Dad could keep picking. If he had to come down from his ladder each time we needed to have our ladder moved, it would cut into his picking time. One of us would position his ladder and hold it while the other would place the third leg near the trunk of the tree for a proper set. With practice, we each eventually acquired the skill and strength needed to move our ladder around the tree in an upright position and set it without help. This improved our productivity a great deal.

Most cherries were picked with the stems on. Before starting, we were taught the proper way to pick without damaging the fruit. We were shown how to reach our forefinger around the stem or group of stems near the branch, grip and twist upward to remove the stems from the branch without putting any pressure on the cherries and without breaking off the spurs, and place the cherries gently in the pail. It took a long time to fill that first pail.

Cherries were picked "by the bucket", or twelve-quart pail. We were paid fifty cents for each pail-full. (Fifty cents was a lot of money in 1944. At that time, thirty-five cents an hour was considered good pay.) "Checker" stands were set up in a central location in the orchard where the workers were picking. Wooden boxes were brought to the location on low flat trailers called "swampers", and picked up later when they were full. Full pails of cherries were carried to the checker station where they were emptied into the boxes. We were given a "ticket" (one-inch by two-inch colored paper with writing on it) for each full pail. The tickets were redeemed at the end of the day.

That beautiful first tree we picked was the closest one in the orchard to the farm buildings. It was an advantage for us because we didn't have far to carry our ladders to begin picking. The "checker" was also close by, so our pails full of cherries only needed to be carried a short distance to be checked in and emptied.

On the very first day, a pattern was established. Dad worked the top of the tree while Mom and "us kids" picked the lower branches. We all did some picking "on the ground" at first, but then left most of that for Mom. It was a good feeling to be there, working together as a family.

From the very beginning, we were in a contest to see who could fill his pail the quickest. Over time, it became an increasingly competitive activity for our family. Although we had no way of knowing at the time, this naturally competitive setting, repeated over and over every day in the orchard, not only influenced what we were to accomplish while picking fruit as a family, but what we were to accomplish individually throughout our lives. It was great training.

The weather was almost perfect every day. It needed to be because, if ripe cherries are rained upon, they split wide open when the sun comes out, and the crop is ruined.

That first day was memorable. By the end of the day, we had picked forty-four pails of cherries from that one tree. We were all exhausted from lifting the heavy ladders, the picking and from carrying the pails of cherries hooked to our harnesses. We fell asleep on the way home. It was a good day!

"YEAH, BUT THERE'S FOURTEEN OF 'EM!"

By the time the cherries were all picked in the George Oliver orchard on "Cherry Hill", the Sloter family was well known. We were in the orchard at "first light" (as early as four-thirty in the morning) every day but Sunday. By the time the checkers and other pickers got there, we usually had all of our pails full of Royal Ann cherries, waiting to be checked in. We never left the orchard before five-thirty or six o'clock in the evening, when the checkers wouldn't take any more cherries.

Our family was very competitive. Every day was a contest in our family and the guy to beat was Dad. He was fast, and a little rough. We had to take "spurs" out of his pails before we could take them to the checker. ("Spurs" are the half-inch-or-so long branches or twigs to which cherries and two or three leaves are attached. They are important for the next year's crop.) In the beginning, we concentrated on which of us could fill his pail first but, as days passed, we began counting how many pails each of us had picked that day.

Dad continued picking the "tops" of the trees while Julian and I picked the "middle". Mom still picked "the bottoms" and some of the "middle". Julian and I soon got much better at handling the ladders and faster at picking, even while doing a "clean" job. We always picked with both hands.

Several times during the day, Dad would holler across the tree and ask, "How many pails do you have, Boys?" Of course, we would tell him. Then he would tell us how many he had. He always had more -- he said. My brother and I worked as fast as we could but we never seemed to gain on Dad. Eventually, we became suspicious. We checked and found out that what Dad picked, and what he told us he had picked, were not always the same. Julian and I were able to keep up with, and sometimes beat, him. Granted, the fruit in the top of the tree is harder to get and it was a long way up and down the ladder for Dad -- but, nevertheless, we were pretty proud to be able to compete so well with Dad when we were just eight and nine years old.

Our contest progressed from trying to beat each other to trying to beat each other *and* the family's total for the previous day. We advanced from picking forty-four pails the first day to over one hundred a day later on. Soon it became our goal to pick one hundred pails each day before going home. Sometimes that was tough to do. Picking conditions varied from tree to tree and "clean-up" time also varied from day to day. All the fruit had to be off a tree before we could leave it. "Stragglers" (scattered fruit in the center of the tree) were awkward to get and consumed a lot of time, but also needed to be picked. The distance to the checker and the distance to our next tree, as well as the distance between the trees (if the trees were too close together, it was hard to move the ladders around the tree we were working on), were also factors. All of these conditions affected our "picking time" and, therefore, how hard we had to work to reach our goal each day.

After we had been picking for about two weeks, we began hearing questions throughout the day from other pickers about how many "pails" we had. Then someone would mention another family and how many "pails" they had. We hadn't paid any attention to other families and how much they picked but, after that, a contest developed over the entire orchard. By that time, we were confident that we could beat any family in the orchard. That was until we heard about a family of seven that "came to pick". Every time we took "pails" to the checker, we heard how many the newcomers had. Sometimes they had more than we did and we wondered how many they had that hadn't been turned in yet.

From time to time, we would hear bits and pieces of conversations about our family. Of all the comments about us that we overheard, our favorite was, "Yeah, but there's fourteen of 'em!"

The family of seven gave us "a run for our money", but we picked right up to the last minute, even after they had quit for the day.

In the end, we were undefeated. No family in the orchard ever picked as much fruit as the Sloters on any given day.

THE STANDARD

Not all fruit trees are created equal. Nor are orchards, or owners, or pruners, or foremen. All of these factors entered into whether picking fruit was fun for us, or just plain hard work. And whether we could earn "good money", or just an average amount.

As the season progressed, we found ourselves comparing every cherry-picking job to "Cherry Hill" and every orchard owner to George Oliver. There were none better. It was our biggest and best job. We came to feel that without being able to work for George Oliver on Cherry Hill, there would be no cherry-picking season for us.

The orchards on Cherry Hill were on the mostly flat to slightly rolling top of a large hill. Setting ladders there was usually not too difficult, except for a few trees that were located on the edge of the orchard where the ground was more sloping. One memorable tree we picked for George Oliver was on more of a side hill than usual with branches hanging over the edge, above a road several feet below. It was about the last tree we picked for George Oliver that year. We were concerned about reaching the outer branches without falling. Dad ended up setting a tall "spike" ladder on the edge of the road to get to all of the fruit. It was risky and quite a struggle, but we managed to finish it without incident.

In a very hilly situation, it is often necessary to position the "leg" of a ladder at an odd angle from the main part of the ladder to end up with a reasonably "safe set". There is always the risk of having a ladder tip over and, since much of the picking is done from near the top of the ladder, a fall could cause serious injury. There were many times, after climbing almost to the top, that a ladder would "start to go". Sometimes we could quickly back down and reset but, at other times, we had to grab a tree branch to keep from tipping and call for someone to steady the ladder while we came down to reset.

If a tree was to produce abundant and good quality fruit, it had to be properly pruned. The best fruit is often in new growth in the top of a tree. If a tree is allowed to grow too tall, it becomes very difficult to reach the best picking. A tree also needs to be "opened up" to allow sunlight to reach all of the branches so the fruit will ripen evenly. It is equally important to prune in such a way that a ladder can be set "inside" the tree during harvest season, so the fruit can be picked without damaging the fruit or the tree. This was accomplished by making sure that no branches crossed each other and that there was enough room between major branches to accommodate a ladder.

Every orchard has a variety of trees and unique situations. Some trees are larger than others, some are on flat ground, some are on a side hill and some are loaded more heavily with fruit than others. Of course, we always wanted to get the best trees and the best situations that we could.

In most orchards in which we worked, a foreman would lead workers to the next tree to be picked. He could choose to give them a "good tree" or a "bad tree", it was up to him. We found that it was always a good idea to "get on the good side" of the foreman because he could make a tremendous difference in how much we could pick.

These were some of the things we learned while picking cherries on Cherry Hill. We found that these basic "rules" applied in all the orchards in which we worked.

TRICKS OF THE TRADE

Picking cherries "by the bucket" involved some variables that could make a considerable difference in the number of buckets picked by the end of the day.

In hurrying to get the pail filled, the natural movement of your arms and body would cause the cherries to settle into the pail. Also, it was impossible to avoid bumping the pail on the ladder and on your knees as you moved quickly up and down the ladder. Additionally, if you left the partially full pail of cherries hooked to your harness while moving your ladder (which you would normally do in order to save picking time) -- this, too, would cause the cherries to "settle". For these reasons, we soon learned that by gently pouring the cherries from the "picked-in" pail into an empty pail, the fruit would "fluff up" on the stems, taking fewer cherries to fill the pail. This little "procedure" would gain us about one pail in ten.

How full is full? Could we get credit for a pail that wasn't absolutely full to the top? We tried and found that we could. Some checkers were more lenient than others. We exploited this variable to the limit. We would leave the cherries as low in the pail as we thought we could get by with until a checker would complain or reject what we delivered. Occasionally the checker would take cherries from one pail to fill the others to an acceptable level.

Sometimes, if the checker was busy, she would allow us to empty our pails into boxes and would then count our empty pails. When this happened, she wouldn't look as closely at how full our pails were. We "helped her out" whenever we could.

I'm not sure if it happened to him by accident the first time or not. But Dad came up with a "system" to take advantage in another way. From time to time, Dad would go to the checker carrying two full pails in each hand and one full pail setting in an empty one hooked to his picking harness. Setting down the four pails in his hands, he would unhook the empty pail containing the full pail and set it on the ground. While the checker was emptying the four pails and setting them on the ground, Dad would separate the two pails that had been hooked to his harness and set the empty with those the checker had emptied. He would then empty the full pail into a box and place that empty pail with the others. The checker would count the six pails and hand Dad six tickets.

Later, Dad had little six-year-old Don do the same thing. Struggling, he would carry one full pail in each hand and one on the harness inside an empty. It worked for him, too. The checker never caught on.

It was the first day of work when Dad pulled off a classic "slight of hand". At the end of the day, he went to redeem the forty-four tickets from the day's work. He handed all of the tickets to the check-out lady and said, "Here, you can count them back to me." She did! While she was counting out his $22 pay, he calmly put the tickets back into his pocket. She paid him and he walked away with not only the day's pay, but also the day's tickets.

Mom hated it when Dad did things like that. She made it clear to "us kids" that it was dishonest and not the thing to do. She told Dad the same thing, but he would just laugh. It seemed to fall on "deaf ears". However, although we knew it wasn't right, we always marveled at Dad's ability to "find an angle" and turn a situation to his advantage. That type of chicanery took place frequently early in our first year, but not later. Maybe it stopped because we became friends with the orchard owners -- or maybe Mom's scolding had some effect on Dad after all.

A PICNIC EVERY DAY

"If you're gonna work, ya gotta eat!"

We began every day with a big breakfast, usually hot "Cream of Wheat" or "Cocoa Wheat". Sometimes we had cold cereal such as corn flakes, Cheerios, puffed wheat or puffed rice. That was a treat for "us kids", but we learned that the hot cereal "stuck to our ribs" better. Whenever we had cold cereal for breakfast, we would be hungry before stopping for our mid-morning lunch break.

The large metal box was always full of sandwiches, carrots, cookies, etc., and the thermos bottle full of coffee, when we started the day. Working on the farm taught Mom and Dad that a short break for a sandwich and something to drink both mid-morning and mid-afternoon, in addition to the noon meal, would enable a person to work harder and longer than waiting until noon or evening to eat. They insisted that we "take a break" and eat something, before we felt hungry.

We looked forward to those breaks as much for the conversation as for the food. Once, when we were preparing to eat, Don said, "Oh boy, a picnic every day." We sat around the "lunch box" on overturned pails and compared notes about how picking was going on our part of the tree and how many pails we had by that time, as well as just plain "chit-chat". Somehow, Dad always seemed to come up with something funny to say, a joke to tell, or something amusing to tell us about. It may not have been a picnic every day, but those were good times.

Dad with his picking bucket.

Mom on a ladder.

SNEAKING UP ON 'EM!

Dad pulled into the apple orchard, parked our 1935 Ford and turned off the engine and headlights. Looking out, we could just make out the shape of the trees against the dawning sky. It was still dark! Dad looked at the trees, then over at Mom on the seat beside him and said, "I didn't know we had to sneak up on the sons-a-bitches." We all had a good laugh and settled back in our seats to wait for daylight. Mom laid her head back on her seat and fell fast asleep. She was still tired.

Our days, working from sun-up until five or six o'clock in the afternoon, were long. But Mom's were much longer. We always stopped for groceries on the way home from work, and Dad usually went in to buy them. Sometimes he would include a "Banana Frosted Stick" treat for each of us. They sure tasted good. Other times, we would stop at DeLormes store on North Fourth Street and Dad would go to a nearby tavern for a beer, while Mom did the shopping. Dad didn't like it if we came into the tavern to get him, so we would sit in the car and wait -- and wait. I'm sure it didn't seem to Dad that he was gone that long but, to us kids, waiting in the car to go home, it seemed like hours. After working in the orchard all day, we were always tired and hungry, and anxious to get home. When Dad would finally return to the car and we could go home, Mom would still have to fix supper. After supper, the kids would do the dishes and go to bed. Mom said we needed our rest. We never protested and had no trouble falling asleep. Whether picking cherries, apricots, plums, peaches, or apples, each picking season was short, so we gave it all we had while it lasted. There was no time or energy for play. Mom was always busy; cooking, cleaning, or washing clothes in an old wringer washer and hanging them out to dry -- even on Sunday -- besides working in the orchard every day during picking season.

"I don't remember sitting down. If I did, I'd fall asleep. It was a tough time."

Mom seldom got to bed before eleven o'clock at night and was generally up by three o'clock in the morning "fixing lunch" and "getting breakfast" before arousing the rest of the family.

Eventually, the strain of that exhausting schedule began to show on Mom. Something had to be done about it! Mom and Dad began planning the evening meals to make them as simple and as easy to prepare as possible. This saved Mom some time and effort in the evenings. Also, Mom stopped packing lunch before we went to work so she wouldn't need to get up so early in the morning. To simplify our eating in the orchard, Mom would put bread, butter, sandwich meat, cheese, peanut butter, jelly, cookies, candy bars, canned fruit drinks and water in a cardboard box to take along. We soon discovered that it not only made things easier for Mom, but that we actually preferred making our own sandwiches. That way, we had more choices and our sandwiches weren't soggy. Before that, Mom would ask if anyone wanted another sandwich and she would hear, "What kind is left?" If it wasn't to our liking, we would pass. It was difficult for her to pack the right amount of everything. Also, when we were picking cherries, plums, peaches, or apples, we could usually find ripe fruit for snacks.

It wasn't long before we began to see a difference in Mom. The springs on Mom and Dad's bed no longer made noise in rhythm with Mom's heartbeat when she was sleeping. She seemed to have more energy and didn't look so "dragged out". Those little changes had made a big difference!

Author picking cherries

SETTING PINS

Somebody at school was talking about "setting pins" to earn money. I didn't know what they were talking about, so I asked. I learned that it was setting bowling pins at the local bowling alley. It paid ten cents a line.

We were in our second year in Yakima, Washington, and Julian and I were in the fifth grade at Barge School. After school one afternoon, we decided to go to the bowling alley to check it out. Mom and Dad knew where we were going so, when the manager told us that we could set pins that night if we wanted to, we jumped at the chance.

Each alley had a setting machine -- a rack -- which had ten slots in which to place the pins. When a lever on the back of the machine was pushed down, the pins in the rack would be mechanically moved to an upright position and placed on spots on the floor. The pins were left standing when the lever was released and the rack moved back up out of the way. It was necessary to place the pins in the rack above where pins had been knocked down and not above standing pins. We were a little slow at first, as we would pick up one pin at a time and place it in the rack. But, before long, we got "the hang of it" and were picking up two pins in each hand, then three, as we gained experience.

We watched as the first bowling balls came speeding down the alley toward where we were sitting on the three-foot-high dividing wall between alleys, wondering which way the pins would fly when the ball hit. Some bowlers would throw the ball extremely hard and the pins would fly wildly around in "the pit". Once in a while, one would even fly out. It was not the safest place to be.

As soon as the ball came to rest in the pit, we would jump down, grab the ball, and send it back to the front on the ball return rails. Then we would gather the downed pins and place them in the rack and climb back on the wall to wait for the next ball. Occasionally, we would hear a ball coming down the alley while we were still in the pit and would have to scramble for safety.

There was a narrow pass-way in the dividing wall between every other alley, which allowed a person to move easily between pits and to "set two alleys". At first, it didn't seem as if we would ever be able to do that. But, by the end of the first week, Julian and I were both "setting two alleys", which made it possible to set as many as one hundred lines working all day Saturday and Saturday night. We consistently earned five or six dollars per night. That was a lot of money in 1946 and it became our goal whenever we worked. We enjoyed the fast pace of league bowling and requested to work "league nights" whenever possible.

Julian and I usually worked on Friday night, all day Saturday, and occasionally on a weeknight during the school year. Mom would prepare food, and Dad would bring it to the bowling alley for us on Friday nights and Saturdays. Sometimes Dad would buy food uptown for us. We especially enjoyed the "Coney Island Red Hot" chilidogs that were sold just down the street from the bowling alley.

Our family had gone to Washington to work and save money. Julian and I wanted do our part to accomplish that goal, so most of the money we earned setting pins was given to our parents to add to our family savings.

OUR PAL -- GONE

It may have been that each thought the other was invading his territory, or maybe they just didn't like each other. Whatever the reason, if they got within twenty feet of each other, there was sure to be a fight.

Blackie, a black, mostly-Cocker Spaniel, with a little white on his chest, belonged to our landlords, Rudy and Viola Pieti. They lived up the hill, three houses west of us, at the end of "O" Street in Yakima, Washington. Soon after we moved into the rental house, Blackie and Pal met up with each other -- and the fight was on. We had seen Pal in fights before, but never with the ferocity displayed as when he met Blackie. We had never seen Pal lose a fight. But, when he and Blackie tore into each other, we weren't sure what would happen. They were nearly the same size and equally determined. They proved to be as even a match as you would ever find. Once they started fighting, there was no stopping them, no matter how we tried. The two dogs had several fights, but there was never a clear winner. They would fight until they were exhausted, then each would go home to lick his wounds. There were no visible scars on Pal; his heavy fur hid them. Blackie nearly lost an eye in one of their early battles and carried that scar for the rest of his life.

One morning, about a week after one of his battles with Blackie, we noticed that Pal wasn't himself. He was cowering under Mom and Dad's bed, then stuck close to Mom most of the day. Otherwise, he would just lie around, or come up to one of us as if he wanted something, and then go lie down again. That evening, a very strange thing happened. He came up to me, whined a little, then opened and closed his mouth. His skull seemed to move up and down on top of his head. He was obviously very ill. Dad loaded Pal in the car and took him to the veterinarian. We were sad and anxious about our special dog, hoping and praying that the vet could help him.

We waited anxiously for Dad and Pal to come home. When Dad finally returned, Pal wasn't with him. He said that the vet needed to keep him overnight.

The next night after school, Dad came home after going to the vet to check on Pal. He said something to Mom, pulled out a chair in the kitchen, and sat down. Then he told us kids to come sit down. Both he and Mom had a sad, concerned look on their faces. We could tell something was wrong and waited for the bad news. Dad explained that the veterinarian had not been able to diagnose Pal's problem, and that there was nothing he could do for him. He had given Pal a shot to "put him to sleep". We all cried and couldn't eat supper that evening Our good friend, Pal, was gone! He had lost his last fight.

SUMMER FUN

It was a Sunday, and Mom and Dad had given Julian and me permission to go to the municipal pool which was about six blocks away. Wearing swim trunks, money in one hand and a towel in the other, we hurried out the door. This was our first trip to the pool and we were really looking forward to it.

It was hot in Yakima in the summer and this particular day was especially hot. The rocks in the alley between our house and Fourth Street hurt our bare feet. We were anxious to get to Fourth Street and the smooth blacktop. However, after only a few steps on the smooth surface, we realized that walking on the blacktop would be like walking on the top of Mom's old cook stove with the fire going! We quickly stepped off the blacktop onto the narrow shoulder to let our feet cool. Unfortunately, there was no sidewalk at the northern end of North Fourth Street. We could either walk on the blacktop, the coarse gravel at the edge of the blacktop, or in one of the steep, slanted ditches that bordered the road on both sides. After waiting three or four minutes, we got back on the blacktop and ran as fast as we could until our feet were burning, then stepped onto the shoulder again. The next time, we ran to where a tree shaded the street. We repeated that process several times on the way to the pool. By the time we got there, our feet were so tender that they hurt even when we walked on the cool, wet surface around the pool.

After getting into the pool, we soon realized that the other kids our age were swimming skillfully, wherever they wanted, even in the deep end. Julian and I would have liked to join in the games of tag, but we couldn't swim. We felt inferior and like outsiders.

Anxious to learn, we watched how the other kids swam, then tried to copy them. They made it look easy, yet it remained very difficult for us. Dad even went to the pool with us and tried to help, but he couldn't swim either. It was like the "blind leading the blind". Dad and Mom would let us go to the pool on Sundays and also when there was no fruit to pick. We went swimming every chance we got that summer, watched closely how the other kids swam, and kept trying.

Eventually, we were able to swim nearly half way across the pool and told Mom and Dad of our progress. The next time we went swimming, Dad went along to watch. Anxious to show Dad what we could do, we jumped into the pool and swam under water until we needed to come up for air, then stood up and waited for his reaction. He smiled and said, "That was pretty good, Boys, but I thought you would swim on top of the water!"

Continuing our efforts that summer, we learned to tread water, then dog paddle and then, finally, to swim with full strokes. By the end of the summer, we had graduated to swimming in the deep end and then in the Yakima River with the "big kids".

The river was closer to our house than the swimming pool, it was always open -- and it was free. We liked swimming there, but we never ventured very far from shore that first summer.

The next summer found us going to the river whenever we wanted to go swimming. We had graduated from swimming in the pool. We liked the feeling of freedom we got from swimming in the river and the challenge presented by the current and the rapids. A strong swimmer could swim upstream in the fastest current and "hold his own", avoiding being carried downstream. That became our new goal and we reached it that year. We had met the challenge.

There were quiet backwaters along the river. Sand washed into the calm, shallow areas, creating ideal swimming holes. One hot summer Sunday, our whole family walked across the pasture to a popular spot to picnic and cool off in the water. A steep drop-off into the fast current bordered the backwater. It was safe enough within about twenty feet of shore but, beyond that, it was very dangerous -- especially to a non-swimmer. Julian and I were the only ones in our family who could swim.

We all got into the water and were enjoying splashing around when suddenly someone shouted, "Where's Donnie?" Looking around, we saw his hand stick up out of the water, then go under. Don was near the fast current where the water started to get deep. He had gotten in over his head!

None of our family was close enough to reach Don before the current would pull him into the main river and sweep him downstream. Luckily, a teenage girl happened to be standing in the water about six feet from where we had seen Don's hand. Having become aware of what was happening, she looked in the direction of the river just as Don stuck his hand up out of the water again. She lunged toward Don, grabbed his arm, and pulled him to safety. To this day, we feel certain that she saved his life.

A tragedy had been averted. We dressed, gathered our things, and went home, very thankful that all of us were together.

After that, Dad and Mom began to think about our swimming, the danger involved, and the energy it required. Dad set Julian and me down and said, "I don't want you guys to go swimming during the picking season. It saps too much strength and you'll be too tired to work the next day. I want you to rest up on Sunday. Besides, swimming in the river looks too risky." We understood what Dad was saying. We could see that swimming in the Yakima River entailed more risk than we had previously thought. We willingly complied with his wishes, which nearly eliminated swimming for us. We would need to find another form of recreation.

THE OFF SEASON

It wasn't easy for Dad to stay busy in the off-season in Yakima, Washington. Even though he pruned fruit trees in the winter, worked with irrigation and thinned apples in the spring, there were times when he couldn't find work. Our income was inconsistent, but expenses continued whether Dad was working or not.

To help pay expenses and preserve our savings, after apple picking was over in the fall, Mom took a job working nights. She worked in a "dehydrator" in Selah, a small community just north of Yakima. Her job was to hand-feed apples, one at a time, into a high-speed machine that cored, peeled, and sliced them, ready to be dried. It required quickness and precise timing to keep the "cups" full and avoid getting a hand or finger caught in the machine.

Mom's co-workers were from that area and considered her an outsider. They resented her having a job there and did everything they could think of to get her to quit. She experienced almost constant harassment.

One night, a lady working next to her made a wrong move and sliced a terrible gash in her hand. Mom, already tense because of the constant harassment, became increasingly nervous and upset. Distracted, and her timing off, she placed an apple in the machine just as it was in the core and peel cycle. The machine closed on one of her thumbs, smashing it and cutting it severely.

Mom was forced to miss several weeks' work while it healed. Dad went to work in Mom's place to hold the job for her. Dad was big and strong, but not nimble like Mom. He had trouble keeping up with the machine. The shift foreman was constantly on the move, watching what was happening on the line. He gave Dad time to catch on and to prove himself. About the third night, after watching Dad fumbling around with his big hands trying to get the apples placed in the "cups" between the machine cycles, he took Dad aside and said, "You're coring the apples in every place but where they should be. Why don't you just go home? We'll hold the job for your wife. She can come back when she is able."

Mom's co-workers who had been harassing her didn't think she would be back. But she was determined that, if and when she left that job, it would be of her own choosing, not because someone else wanted her to leave. When her thumb was healed enough, Mom went back to work.

Mom tried going back to the high-speed machines. But, because of her injury, she was just too nervous, worrying that it might happen again. It was about that time that management decided to close the night shift. All but three people working that shift were laid off. Mom, along with two other ladies, one of whom was a redhead like Mom, was moved to the day shift and given a job away from the coring/peeling machines, sorting out substandard apple slices as they passed by on a conveyer belt. The fact that others were laid off and Mom was kept on infuriated some of the day-shift workers. Just as they were leaving for the day, a large woman slapped Mom. She was crying when Dad came to pick her up. Mom felt like giving up and quitting. Dad said, "Don't let them buffalo you. Don't give in." When Mom went to work the next day, the woman, who had slapped her, looked at Mom and said, "You're back again? I didn't think you'd be back." Mom said, "Well, I am." That marked the end of the harassment. Her co-workers accepted her and that she was there to stay, no matter what. Mom felt good about having "stuck it out".

GETTING FIRED

We had been in Yakima for a year and things were going quite well. Dad told Mom's brother (Uncle James) back in Iowa about the money we were making. It sounded good to him and he began to dream of earning good money and saving a "nest egg" himself. He told Dad that he would like to move to Yakima, but he didn't have enough money to make the move and didn't have a car. Dad agreed to loan Uncle James money for the trip and sent him one hundred dollars (a lot of money at that time). Uncle James and his family moved out from Iowa on the train. Dad helped them find jobs picking fruit and gave them a ride to work each day until they earned enough to buy a car.

During the summer, we would begin the harvest season by picking cherries – followed by plums, apricots, peaches, pears and, finally, apples in the fall. There were times between some of those crops when we didn't have work.

Hops, which look like one-inch-long pinecones and are used to flavor beer, are also grown in Yakima Valley. The harvest season for hops falls between some of the fruit crops. Dad thought picking hops would make a good "fill-in" while waiting for the next fruit crop to be ready for picking.

Now, picking fruit was hard work, but not unpleasant -- and we earned good money doing it. Hops were another story. They grew on vines, which wound around cord strings strung from the ground to wires about twelve feet off the ground. Poles, set in rows spaced about eight feet apart, supported the wires. When hops were harvested, a knife attached to a long pole was used to reach up and cut the strings at the wire, allowing the vines to fall to the ground. The hops were then picked off the vines by hand.

Hops weigh like feathers, and we were paid by the pound. We sat in the hot sun by the hour, picking into the tall baskets, then would empty the full baskets into enormous burlap bags. We would pick and pick, but it seemed to take forever to fill those bags. It was impossible to earn decent money. To us kids, it was a really miserable job. We were sure there couldn't be a worse job anywhere.

I was eleven years old and my cousin, Arnie, was nine when our parents found a job picking hops where our families worked side by side. Every day was the same, miserably hot and dry. By the third day, the dust on the paths beside the fields was so deep that we would sink in to our ankles. I couldn't help but sympathize with Arnie when I heard him say, over and over, "I hope we get fired, I hope we get fired." I hated that job, too, but I wasn't sure I wanted us to get fired. Uncle James, a wiry, red-haired, hot-tempered man, listened to Arnie's chant about getting fired until he couldn't stand it any longer. Finally, completely out of patience, he came over to Arnie and "whaled the tar out of him". He really "let him have it"! When finished, Uncle James said, "There, damn it, you're fired! Now get to work!"

Looking back on the experience, I don't think our parents enjoyed picking hops any more than we did. When the bags were full, we took them to the checker to be weighed and got a ticket for the weight. At the end of the day, Dad would turn the tickets in and collect our pay.

As I've referenced several times, Dad was a big, strong man who would always do his best to come out ahead in a less-than-desirable situation. While Mom and us kids were carefully picking each little hop and putting it into our baskets, Dad would grab a vine and strip everything off into his basket, leaves and all, then pour it all into the bag. When he would get his bag full, which wouldn't take long, he would bend down a few times and scoop up soil with both hands and toss it into the bag, too. He would then pour water over the soil and hops to increase the weight. Mom protested to Dad about what he was doing and said more than once, "Bill, you shouldn't do that." But Dad kept it up.

Near the end of the day, someone from the processing plant came to the field and walked over to where we were working. I don't know how he was able to locate the source of the "rough" bags, but I heard him tell Dad, "My God, man, you're putting in everything but the poles!" Dad straightened up from his work and, with a crooked smile, looked down at the man. Nothing more was said; the man turned and walked away.

We didn't go back the next day.

GOING HOME

With Mom working nights, it became Dad's responsibility to wake us kids, prepare breakfast, and get us off to school. We usually had Cream of Wheat, Cocoa Wheat or Malt-O-Meal for breakfast. Our hot cereal was always smooth and creamy when Mom cooked it. But when Dad cooked it, the cereal contained huge lumps. Most were about the size of grapes, but some would fill a teaspoon. We complained at first, but it did no good. Dad was trying, but he just didn't "have the knack". So, we stopped complaining and ate what he prepared.

We liked Yakima. The weather was mild, there were good schools and we had friends there. But most of our relatives were in Iowa. We missed them, and we missed the cornfields and the wide-open spaces. Gradually, we began to long for Iowa. Iowa was still home! Even though we earned good money in Yakima during the cherry-picking and apple-picking seasons, the rest of the year was spent trying to avoid dipping into our savings. We didn't like to have Mom working nights or the fact that sometimes Dad was out of work. We talked and thought more and more about "moving back", but continued to work hard during the picking seasons. We were in Washington to earn money and build our financial reserves. We weren't about to slack off.

Julian and I got stronger and faster with each picking season. By the time we were twelve and thirteen years of age, we could pick as much fruit as a man. The contests between us continued and became more intense. In the end, there was no clear winner. Every now and then someone would tell us about a fast fruit picker of whom they had heard. They were always very, very fast -- and always somewhere else. There was never a man in the orchards where we worked that we couldn't out-pick.

However, our enthusiasm for living and working in Yakima began to wane. We made two trips back to Iowa to visit during the time we lived in Yakima and those trips only added to our desire to return. It was 1948 and we had been in Yakima for four years when the decision was made. We would move back after apple picking season that year. We had money saved, possibly enough to start farming.

We were going home to Iowa!

DECISIONS

When we arrived home in Iowa that fall, Dad went to see George Oxley, a farm manager whom my parents had known for years, and asked him what he thought of starting farming at that time. George was not optimistic about the future of farming and discouraged Dad. George told Dad that the cost of starting would be high and the risk too great. Dad and Mom discussed it at length and decided not to risk losing the money we had worked so hard to save. They still remembered how their parents, on both sides, had struggled and lost in farming.

Having made that decision, Dad went looking for a job. He found employment working for Earl Chambers on his farm four miles west of Corwith. Dad was well-qualified for the job. He needed to earn a living and took the job for the sake of his family, but with little real desire. We moved into a tenant house a mile east across the field from the Chambers' farmstead.

Julian and I also worked for Earl Chambers during school vacation in the summer. We drove tractors cultivating corn and beans, mowing and raking hay, and spreading manure on the fields. We also stacked hay bales in the barn during haying season. We occasionally helped Dad with chores, milking cows and cleaning the barn.

A little extra money came in with Julian and me working in the summer, but that wasn't the most important thing to Dad. He missed the challenges, flexibility, and feeling of self-worth that came from being "on his own". He just couldn't get satisfaction from working for someone else.

In August, 1949, after less than a year working on the Chambers' farm, Dad gave notice and left that job. My parents paid two thousand dollars for a house on the south edge of Corwith. Dad built a chicken house on the back part of the lot for our three hundred chickens and we moved to town.

Don, Julian, and I attended the school where I had started kindergarten and where Mom had graduated from high school in 1932. Don was in fourth grade and Julian and I were in seventh. Corwith Consolidated School was much different from the schools in Yakima. Washington Junior High School in Yakima was much like a college campus. Each class had a home room and we would go to different rooms and different buildings for the various subjects. Also, we had a choice of several subjects in the Yakima schools. Junior high in Corwith, which consisted of the seventh and eighth grades, was in one room. We stayed in that room for all classes. My biggest disappointment was the absence of art, architectural drawing and a well-equipped woodworking shop.

I really missed those things. But, for many reasons, I was happy to be back home in Iowa.

LIFE IN CORWITH

After moving to our house in Corwith, Dad seemed more like himself again. He didn't have a steady job, but he was always able to come up with some way to earn a living. He was on his own and much more at peace with himself.

There weren't many sheep shearers around and plenty of sheep to shear. Having had some experience in that work, Dad decided to become a sheep shearer. He bought the necessary equipment and advertised for work. The calls came in immediately. He wasn't swamped, but was busy enough for a man who wasn't skilled in the work or "toughened in". He understood that time was money, though, so he worked hard to develop his skill and become more proficient.

There was another sheep shearer, Lynell Clapsaddle, who worked in the same general area as Dad. Occasionally their paths would cross and they would visit. Dad soon realized that Lynall was a skilled professional and that he could learn from him. Lynall was a smaller man than Dad, but could shear as many as one hundred and twenty-five sheep a day and go home early. That really impressed Dad. He was struggling through long days and still couldn't shear one hundred sheep a day. Dad began making it a point to stop in whenever he heard that Lynall was in the area. Lynall became the teacher and Dad, the student. They also became good friends. Whenever they got together, whether it was where Dad was shearing or where Lynall was shearing, Lynall would give Dad pointers. Although Dad never felt that he could match Lynall, he became a lot more proficient and confident in his sheep-shearing ability.

Dad bought an old "Big Ben" alarm clock and placed it where it could be seen while he was shearing. He then timed himself with every sheep. After catching and "setting" the sheep, Dad wanted to turn it loose, shorn, in three minutes or less. He began setting goals for each day and for each job, as well as for each sheep. As his proficiency and endurance increased, he found himself attaining his goals more easily. He was eventually able to get his one-hundred-plus sheep a day, if they were all located in one place.

As Dad's shearing skills improved, he began to realize that he could do much more if he wasn't required to use his time and energy catching the sheep and tying the wool. Having someone along to help "set up" his equipment and then "tear it down" when the job was finished would also make quite a difference. Mom was elected. She went with Dad during the week, then Julian or I would go along on Saturdays and during school breaks, so Mom could stay home. Shearing proved to be a good business for Dad and Mom. They made good money, but it was seasonal.

Fruit picking still looked good to Dad and Mom. Dad referred to it as "picking money off trees". They decided we would travel the eighteen hundred miles from Corwith to Yakima to pick fruit after shearing sheep in the spring. We earned good money at that, too, so a pattern was established -- sheep shearing in the spring, fruit picking in the summer, then back to Corwith before school started in the fall. Sometimes Mom and Dad would stay in Washington to pick apples and would send us kids home by ourselves to start school.

I was fifteen years old and a freshman in high school when our family increased once again. Our brother, Dean, was born in April, 1950. Traveling to Yakima to pick fruit was out of the question that year, but was resumed the next. Dean was taken along to the orchard when he was a toddler and was put in a playpen. It was extra work taking him along, but it was the best solution to caring for him.

Eventually, I got a steady job and stayed home in Corwith, while the others "went west". The variety and freedom of our unusual lifestyle suited my parents. They enjoyed the times between seasons when they could catch up on things at home and repair shearing equipment in preparation for the next year.

Time passed and things changed. Eventually it became impractical to go west to pick fruit as the method of payment for picking had changed to paying "by weight". It worked out to be much less than before. As wool prices dropped off, so did the number of sheep in Iowa. Sheep shearing was no longer profitable. What had been two good sources of income had dried up.

Once again, Dad worked at a variety of jobs, including mechanic work for a car dealer in Kanawha, and working at Winnebago Industries, a travel trailer and motorhome factory in Forest City, as well as occasionally working for local farmers.

I was married with two children and living in Forest City, Iowa, when I got a call from Dad. There was excitement in his voice. Dad and Mom occasionally asked my opinion when they were trying to make a decision. This was one of those times. Dad had been working on a large farm, repairing and painting the buildings. He had been using a rented airless paint sprayer and was amazed at how much painting he could do in a short time. He told me how he had put a coat of paint on an entire corncrib in an hour. That experience made

Dad and Mom think about starting a business painting farm buildings. They had checked on the going rate for contract painting and the potential looked good to them. But they wanted to know what I thought before they made the final decision.

Dad and Mom had done their homework before calling me, and I knew a little about the painting business, too. The cost of equipment seemed reasonable considering the potential return on investment and the opportunity it would provide. By the time our conversation ended, I told Dad, "It sounds good to me -- I think you should do it."

Mom and Dad worked together as a team, each one's skills complementing the other. Dad was the strong one who cleaned and painted the high areas and Mom was the "support crew" who kept paint in the airless sprayer pump and did the "fine painting" of trim and around windows. Together, they did top-quality work. Mom also did "the figuring" to successfully bid jobs. They were in demand from the start and continued in that profession for many years.

Being a professional farm-building painter required handling tall, heavy ladders and constant climbing. That type of work, and the hard work Dad had done all his life, eventually took its toll. Dad's legs began to "give out" and he had trouble setting and climbing the ladders. Dad and Mom didn't know what to do. They even considered quitting the painting business, but didn't know what they would do for income if they did?

Dad and Mom told me what was happening and again wondered what I thought. I pondered their dilemma for a few days, then offered a possible solution. I had taken an old pickup in trade in my business. I could build a two-level, sixteen-foot-long scaffold on it. One level would be six feet off the ground and the other twelve and one-half feet, both extending the full length of the pickup. A short extension ladder would be mounted on the top scaffold with hinges to make reaching the high peaks of the buildings much easier and safer. It would be a stable, self-propelled scaffold, which would eliminate ninety percent of their ladder handling and climbing. The investment would be very low, especially considering what it could do for them. There was no hesitation. They liked the idea immediately and wanted the project completed as soon as possible. The original goal in building the scaffold was to extend the time my parents could paint by two or three years. As it turned out, although they gradually began to slow down, that piece of equipment enabled them to continue painting for another eight years.

THE POOL HALL

Dad enjoyed stopping at the "pool hall" for a beer or two and to "shoot the breeze with the boys" on the way home from work. Occasionally some interesting things happened during those stops. Dad had a reputation for having a good sense of humor and for being a "rough and tough" character. That would cause some of the other patrons to challenge him from time to time. It was almost always in good-natured fun, such as pulling fingers or arm wrestling. The loser would buy the beer. But, occasionally, someone would make the mistake of saying something that Dad would take as an insult and "all hell would break loose".

Once, a smaller man than Dad, whom Dad didn't know, challenged him to a wrestling match and included an insult. Dad had been shearing sheep all day, handling two-hundred-pound sheep in the process. He wasn't interested in games and was in no mood to let an insult pass by unaddressed. The challenge was answered in an instant with the challenger being lifted off his feet and hurled through the air over the billiard scorekeeping wire, more than seven feet off the floor. Dad turned back to the bar and finished his drink. The other man lay on the floor for some time, then finally got to his feet and limped out.

Another time, in the same pool hall, and again after having sheared all day, Dad was standing at the bar having a beer when someone came up behind him and said, "Move over and make room for a man." Dad moved over, but the man wouldn't need the room. Dad backhanded him and he was out on the floor. The bartender said, "You might have broken his neck, Bill." Dad said, "No, I didn't hit him that hard, he'll be okay." Dad picked up his beer, walked across the room, and sat in a booth with some friends. The man on the floor woke up a few minutes later, picked himself up, looked around as if he didn't know where he was or what had happened, and stumbled out of the pool hall.

Someone else, who was taller and heavier than Dad, went over to the booth where Dad was setting, looked down at him in a challenging way and said, "I'm scared." Looking up, Dad said, "I don't want any trouble, go sit down." The man became more belligerent and repeated, "I'm scared." Dad got up out of the booth, stepped up close to the man pestering him and said, "Go sit down and leave me alone." The man moved closer to Dad and again said, "I'm scared." The two men were toe to toe and the other man never saw the short, powerful jab coming. Out on his feet, he crumpled to the floor.

"I just gave him a little tap on the button."

Dad was not easily frightened, but he was one night after dark in Los Angeles, California. He was there visiting his brother, Earl, and went out after dark to buy something. As Dad was returning to Earl's apartment, someone came out of an alley and approached him. Whether the man meant Dad any harm or not, we will never know. The man was found the next morning with several broken bones in his face. Dad hadn't waited to find out what the man wanted. His reaction had been instant, hitting the man in the face with all the strength he had. Dad had learned long ago, in the interest of self-defense, to strike first and ask questions later.

Dad was a man who enjoyed a good laugh and enjoyed giving others a good laugh, as well. One evening he came home after he had been at the pool hall and went to the basement where he kept his sheep-shearing equipment. He came upstairs carrying his hand-held electric sheep-shearing clippers. Mom asked, "What are you going to do with that?" "Sherl wants a haircut," he said, and walked out the door. Dad and Sherl had been standing at the bar talking when Sherl said he had to leave to get a haircut. But he didn't leave, he decided to have another beer first. By the time he finished the beer, the barber shop had closed. Dad offered to give Sherl a haircut with his sheep shears. To Dad's surprise and delight, Sherl agreed. Dad left to get his equipment. Back at the pool hall, Dad plugged in the clipper, took hold of Sherl, put him on the floor and held him between his knees like he would a sheep. By this time, other activity stopped and all eyes were on Dad and Sherl. Holding an ear in one hand to keep from cutting it off and the clipper in the other, Dad ran the clipper over Sherl's head, leaving his hair about a quarter-inch long. In the process, the clipper pulled the skin up and scraped it in places. The next day, Sherl showed up with small scabs on his head. That little antic was good for a laugh that night and for a long time to come. I still hear the story told from time to time when Dad's name comes up.

Dad was a somewhat talented ventriloquist, too. He ordered a Charlie McCarthy doll and had a good time with that at the pool hall, again enjoying giving others a good laugh.

As we kids grew to adulthood, we were always amazed at Dad's strength and stamina, even in his later years. We remember mostly, though, how he enjoyed a good laugh and how he could laugh at himself.

TRAGEDIES

Even though my parents had their rolling scaffold, they couldn't use it all the time. Painting farm buildings and houses still required some climbing. Mom always felt uneasy when Dad was on a roof, as was required when painting a cupola on a barn or corncrib. They would always take special precautions, such as positioning a ladder on the roof with special hooks over the peak to keep it in place. Also, Dad would tie the end of a long rope around his waist and throw the other end over the roof. Mom would anchor it to something on the ground. But even making those preparations was difficult and dangerous. It was necessary to carry the hook ladder onto the roof and to reposition it several times before the painting of a cupola was completed. Being on a roof was the most risky part of any painting job, especially the high barn roofs.

"I would worry all night about Bill having to paint a cupola the next day."

On the day Dad lost his balance, he was standing on the porch roof, painting the gable end of the house. He was twenty feet off the ground and all he could do was jump. It wasn't a choice he wanted to make, but at least he would land on his feet. When he jumped, Dad did land on his feet, which prevented internal or head injuries, but his weight of two hundred ten pounds was too much for his right leg and it broke in several places, below the knee.

That accident was the third in a series of tragic and near tragic occurrences in our family in a relatively short time. Mom was fifty-three years old when she began having health problems in 1968. She had two surgeries in December of that year. First, she had bladder surgery, then major surgery to remove a large abdominal tumor. A third surgery was necessary six weeks later to reverse a colostomy. We thought for a while that we might lose Mom, especially when the doctors suspected cancer. Mom's response to the possibility of cancer was, "If its cancer, just let me die."

Following the second surgery, Mom said, "I thought maybe this time wouldn't be so bad. But it was just as bad as the first. I don't want to ever go through that again." Following the surgery, we watched as Mom healed, grew stronger and gained weight. She had been quite thin before. We had attributed it to hard work, but maybe the large benign tumor was to blame. Her health gradually improved and eventually seemed better than ever.

Four months later, our youngest brother, Dean, age nineteen, was killed in a car accident. Grief gripped the whole family for a long time. Life is so precious, and yet so fragile. We had lost a loving member of our family. Dean was buried in the Corwith Cemetery, east of town, with a ceramic picture of his handsome young face adorning the tombstone.

It was a couple months later, while we were still grieving the loss of Dean, that Dad fell. His leg was set and put in a cast that reached from his toes to his upper thigh. He was completely immobilized. Dad's leg needed time to heal and the painting job needed to be finished. There would be no pay until it was done. My parents were owed for both paint and labor. They needed the money! Mom hired another contract painter to paint the "high stuff" while she worked on the windows and trim, as she had been doing when the accident occurred.

Mom's working to finish up the painting meant that she was out of the house during the day and Dad was left alone. He couldn't go anywhere or do anything, so he chose to watch television. Eventually he tired of that and turned it off. That left him alone with his thoughts. He thought about Dean. Dad was overwhelmed with grief over the loss of his youngest son, and the thought that he had also nearly lost his wife most likely contributed to his anguish.

Dad began hallucinating, claiming that he had talked to Dean, had seen Jesus, had new teeth coming in, and that a tree was sprouting from his head. He suffered a complete mental breakdown. My family and I were gone for the weekend when it happened. Mom called Julian and he took action, taking Dad to the University of Iowa Hospital in Iowa City for treatment. Dad was fifty-nine years of age at the time.

Dad's condition proved to be a difficult case for the doctors. Eventually, however, he did respond to treatment and was discharged from the hospital. Mom and a friend drove to Iowa City and brought him home. The medication Dad was on when he left the hospital caused side effects that Mom wasn't familiar with, so when he staggered from the car to the house after they arrived home, she wasn't concerned. Mom thought she was seeing a side effect from the medication. She learned later that he had suffered a stroke. Dad's health problems began to compound. After several months of recovery time, however, Dad and Mom were able to resume painting.

The broken leg, past injuries and mental problems took their toll on Dad. Various medications were tried before one was found that would more or less keep things stable for him. Mom learned to adjust dosages to keep his condition in balance, but it was a delicate balance.

Dad suffered more mental breakdowns and small strokes over the years that followed. Many different medications were tried with limited, and sometimes negative, results. The only thing left to try was shock treatments. The results were amazing. That became the treatment of choice. It was quick, effective, and had few side effects. From then on, whenever Dad got to the point where he needed help, shock treatment was used.

My parents struggled to earn a living after Dad's mental breakdown and stroke and, as time passed, it became increasingly difficult. Dad just couldn't work like he used to. Finally, when Dad turned sixty-two, they contacted the Social Security Administration and began drawing Social Security.

"It was a Godsend."

DAD'S LAST DAYS

As time passed, Dad's health problems seemed to compound. He was in and out of the hospital and needed more and more care at home. Dad's mental and physical condition varied between stable and needing hospital care. Mom was the "primary care giver" and was more or less "on duty" twenty-four hours a day, seven days a week. The load that placed on her became almost unbearable.

Even though Mom was small, she was strong and stood up amazingly well under the stressful load. Adding to her stress, Dad seemed to resent her good health and strength and began to verbally abuse her. Yet, he was completely dependent upon her for everything. It never made sense, but I guess you can't make sense of mental illness.

To complicate things even further, Dad was not a candidate for a rest home. His mental condition prevented that. And he was not a candidate for a mental hospital. His physical condition prevented that. Fortunately, Mom, being close to the situation and with the help of the doctors, was able to keep Dad's mental condition relatively stable by adjusting the dosage of his various medications.

Dad was eighty-two when he entered the hospital for the last time. In a rational moment, still displaying his sense of humor, though gravely ill, he said, "If I'd known I was going to live so long, I'd have taken better care of myself." Lying there in his hospital bed surrounded by family members, he was cracking jokes and laughing, smiling his crooked smile and seemingly enjoying the moment. His final words to me were, "I love you, but you're not pretty enough to kiss."

Somewhat later, when Julian got word that Dad was in the hospital and not expected to live, he made the trip from Atlanta, Georgia (where he lived at the time) to Mason City, Iowa, to see him. As Julian entered the hospital, he met Don's son, Bryan, coming out. Bryan told Julian that Dad was failing, that he was slipping into and out of consciousness and wasn't always lucid. Julian entered Dad's hospital room and stood at his bedside. Dad's eyes were closed. After a while, he opened them and looked up at Julian. Neither spoke. Wondering if Dad recognized him, Julian asked, "Do you know who I am?" Still showing his sense of humor, even on his deathbed, Dad replied, "You're Julian, do you know who I am?"

In those final days of Dad's life, he was shuttled between the physical and mental departments of the hospital, each saying they weren't equipped to handle the other condition. He died in his sleep on February 22, 1993, at age 82.

It was during the last ten or twelve years of Dad's life that I was told many of the stories about his life that are related in this book.

Even in Dad's last years, he had exceptional strength in his arms and hands. From time to time, I would rub his back to help him to relax and to show him that I cared. Even then, his back was still a mass of muscle that had been developed over the many years of hard physical labor.

As I look back and think of Dad, and consider some of the circumstances and events that helped to shape his life and his character, I marvel at what he was able to accomplish. The odds were against him from the start. His very limited "country school" education, coming from a family of fourteen children, and being on his own at age thirteen, presented countless challenges. Yet he made it -- and he did it "his way". He had the courage and fortitude to follow his dreams and the resourcefulness and staying power to overcome incredible obstacles. He cared for his family, and both he and Mom worked ceaselessly to provide for us. He and Mom raised us to know the value of hard work and to always do our best -- to dream and to follow our dreams. It may not have always appeared so by some of Dad's antics, but both Dad and Mom taught us to be honest and fair in our dealings with others and to always pay what we owed. Even though money was often "in short supply" in our family, our parents always paid their bills. No one ever came to our door to "collect".

It was no surprise to our parents, or to us, that we all became successful in our work and in raising our own families. They taught us by their example. We knew they were proud of us, because it showed. They rejoiced in our successes -- they were our inspiration. I have written this book as a tribute to them, and to honor them and their memory. The title of the book, **Uphill All the Way,** is really the story of their lives in a nutshell. They had a hill to climb. But they never stopped climbing -- and they took us with them.

POST SCRIPT

When I completed the first manuscript of this book, Mom was eighty-four years old and in quite good health. Her mind was still sharp, and she maintained her great sense of humor. She was of tremendous help to me as we worked our way through each vignette. The time we spent together in this effort enriched my life beyond measure.

As Mom and I talked and reminisced, I began to think how much fun it would be to take Mom on the same trip our family had taken in 1944. It had been such an unforgettable adventure and pivotal point in our lives that I wanted to relive it with Mom and Marsha. I presented the idea to Marsha and was delighted at her positive response. When Mom heard what we were thinking, she was a little hesitant at first because of her age, but soon warmed to the idea and thought it sounded like fun. With that, I began arranging to make this trip really special. After several phone calls to the state of Washington, I learned that George Oliver had died and that his daughter Muriel inherited the orchard. Loren and Muriel Wintersheid now own and manage the orchard where we had worked on Cherry Hill in the 1940s, but they live in Seattle. I contacted Muriel and she agreed that we should come to Cherry Hill when the cherries would be ready to pick in June 1999. A letter to The Dunlap Fire Station where we had spent the stormy night in 1944 was answered with welcoming response. We could visit there in June. Also, I located an old friend of the family, in Washington, that Mom had mentioned wanting to see again and arranged to see her. Finally, I contacted my retired cousin, Arnie Jackson in Yakima. He and his wife would welcome a visit from us. The stage was set. As time got closer, Mom began to have trouble with pain in a hip and said that we should go without her. My response was that there was no turning back, the trip was for her. We never heard any more about that.

On the morning of May 27, 1999, we loaded Mom's personal items in our motorhome at Mom's little home in Corwith. I could see the look of anticipation on Mom's face as she settled into the seat beside me and fastened her seat belt. There was no question, she was happy to be going. Determined to follow the same roads we had taken in 1944, we drove eleven miles southeast to Kanawha and left from the exact spot we had started from in Feb. 1944. Our first stop was in Dunlap and the fire station. We were welcomed with open arms. The firemen moved equipment out so we could drive our motorhome

158

inside for the night. That evening, some firemen and the son of the policeman who was on duty that night in 1944 came to visit. The next morning, the Fire chief brought us juice and rolls for breakfast. When we left, Mom said; "They treated us like royalty. Nobody will treat us that nice anywhere else." Our visit was featured in the Dunlap Reporter.

As we traveled west on The Lincoln Highway (HWY 30 and sometimes I 80) we made numerous stops to visit museums and special attractions along the way, such as: Lincoln Memorial Highway historic markers, Old West Museum, Tree Rock, Oregon Trail center, (ruts and all), etc. We looked for the infamous Highway 6 shortcut, but never found it. Arriving in Yakima eight days later, we enjoyed Arnie and Jeanne's hospitality and tours around Yakima and Mt. Rainier National Park.

The cherries weren't ready when we went to Cherry Hill on June 9, but Muriel and Loren made an extra effort to be there to meet us anyway. We spent a pleasant day with them, including a meal—more special treatment.

We visited friends from long ago and members of the Jackson family, still living in the area, before heading east toward home. The Lewis and Clark Trail, Yellowstone National Park, Buffalo Bill Historical Center, Jewel Cave, The Black Hills, Mount Rushmore, Wall Drug, The Badlands, and The Corn Palace were among the scenic places we visited on our way back to Iowa. Mom commented: "I bet you never have done so much on a trip before."

Even though Mom's health had begun to fail, she rose to the occasion and seemed to get stronger as we went. She thoroughly enjoyed the experience, as did we. After arriving home, Marsha put together a memory photo-book to make it easier for Mom to share the experience with her friends.

Following is a family update as of August 2003:

Dean, the youngest, had graduated from high school and was working for Allied Mills in Omaha, Nebraska, when he was tragically killed in a car accident in May 1969. He was nineteen.

Sandra married Robert Whitehurst and has one daughter, Lori (Husband: Dan) and two granddaughters -- McKenna, age 10, and Madison, age 7. Her husband, Bob, died of cancer in January 1998 and Sandy, now retired, lives in Clear Lake, Iowa.

Don married Paula Karnatz and they have four children – Patrick (Child: Garret, 12), Barry (Wife: Chuve, Child: Kevin, 7), Bryan (Children: Nikole, 16, and Hanna, 1) and Donald II. Now divorced, Don lives in Omaha, Nebraska, and makes a living in real-estate rental properties.

Julian married Marlene Stover and they have five children – Dennis (Wife: Maureen), David (Wife: Judy; Children: Brad, 16, and Megan, 14), Doug, Daryl (Wife: Michelle; Children: Kyle, 9, and Jordan, 7) and Diane (Husband: Jeff; Children: Bayley, 7, and Ryan, 4). Julian taught high school English and coached high school baseball and basketball before joining IDS (now American Express), where he advanced to the position of Vice President of the Southeast Region. He and Marlene are retired and live in Naples, Florida.

James, Author. I married Marsha Prior and we had two children, Daniel and Michael. Sadly, we lost Dan in an unfortunate accident in August 1980. Mike and his wife, Karen, have three children – Katie, 16, Taylor, 13, and Justin, 8. I became an auto mechanic by trade and eventually owned a conglomerate service station/bulk-plant/auto repair business, specializing in imported auto repair. Now retired, Marsha and I live in Algona, Iowa.